D0565576

cakes from scratch
in half the time

cakes from scratch in half the time

recipes that will change the way you bake cakes forever

by **Linda West Eckhardt**

photographs by **James Baigrie**

CHRONICLE BOOKS
SAN FRANCISCO

Text copyright © 2005 by Linda West Eckhardt.

Photographs copyright © 2005 by James Baigrie.

All rights reserved. No part of this book may be reproduced
in any form without written permission from the publisher.

Library of Congress Cataloging-in-Publication Data available.

ISBN 0-8118-4240-1

Manufactured in China.

Prop styling by Lynda White
Food styling by Stephana Bottom
Photo Assistant: Cheryl Zibisky
Designed by Brooke Johnson
Typeset in New Clear Era and Avenir

Distributed in Canada by Raincoast Books
9050 Shaughnessy Street
Vancouver, BC V6P 6E5

10 9 8 7 6 5 4 3 2 1

Chronicle Books LLC
85 Second Street
San Francisco, California 94105

www.chroniclebooks.com

Ah!Laska Baker's Cocoa is a registered trademark of Donna Maltz; Baby Ruth candy bar is a registered trademark of Nabisco, Inc.; Bacardi Gold rum and Bacardi Ocho rum are registered trademarks of Bacardi and Company, Ltd.; Baker's Joy is a registered trademark of Alberto-Culver Co.; Barbie is a registered trademark of Mattel, Inc.; Bundt pan is a registered trademark of Northland Aluminum Products, Inc.; Butterfinger candy bar is a registered trademark of Societe des Produits Nestle S.A.; Chambord is a registered trademark of Chatam International Inc.; Chatfield's Premium Cocoa Powder is a registered trademark of Tree of Life, Inc.; Coco Lopez is a registered trademark of Empresas La Famosa, Inc.; Dean & DeLuca Bensdorp Cocoa is a registered trademark of Dean & Deluca Brands, Inc.; Droste Cocoa is a registered trademark of Droste B.V.; Fauchon cocoa is a registered trademark of Fauchon S.A.; Frangelico is a registered trademark of Giorgio Barbero & Figli SPA; Ghirardelli Chocolate is a registered trademark of Ghirardelli Chocolate Co.; Guittard chocolate is a registered trademark of Guittard Chocolate Co.; Green & Black's Fairtrade Organic Cocoa is a registered trademark of Green & Black's Limited; Hamilton Beach is a registered trademark of Hamilton Beach, Inc.; Hershey's Cocoa, Hershey's Chocolate, and Hershey's Kisses are registered trademarks of Hershey Foods Inc.; Ibarra chocolate is a registered trademark of Chocolatera de Jalisco, S.A. DE C.V.; Ikea is a registered trademark of Inter-Ikea Systems B.V.; Just Whites is a registered trademark of Deb-El Foods Corporation; Kahlua is a registered trademark of The Kahlua Co.; Kitchenaid is a registered trademark of Whirlpool Properties, Inc.;

La Maison du Chocolat is a registered trademark of La Maison Du Chocolat; Le Creuset cooking ironware is a registered trademark of Le Creuset Societe Anonyme; Lindt 70% Excellence chocolate is a registered trademark of Chocoladefabriken Lindt & Sprungli AG; Microplane grater is a registered trademark of Grace Manufacturing, Inc.; Nabisco Famous Cocoa Wafers are a registered trademark of Nabisco, Inc.; Nestlé Toll House Baking Cocoa is a registered trademark of Societe des Produits Nestle S.A.; Nordic Ware is a registered trademark of Northland Aluminum Products, Inc.; Payday candy bar is a registered trademark of Leaf, Inc.; Pillsbury flour and Pillsbury Bake-Off are registered trademarks of The Pillsbury Co.; Reese's peanut butter chips is a registered trademark of Homestead, Inc.; Rice Krispies are a registered trademark of Kellogg Co.; Saco Premium Cocoa is a registered trademark of Saco Foods, Inc.; Schokinag Christopher Norman cocoa is a registered trademark of Christopher Norman Chocolates (New York), Ltd.; Silpat is a registered trademark of ETS Guy Demarle; Softasilk flour is a registered trademark of General Mills, Inc.; Swans Down flour is a registered trademark of The Girod Corporation; Teflon is a registered trademark of E.I.Dupoint DeMours & Co.; Tobler chocolate is a registered trademark of Aktiengesellschaft Chocolat Tobler; Valrhona chocolate and cocoa powder are registered trademarks of Valrhona S.A.; White Lily flour is a registered trademark of The White Lily Foods Co.

DEDICATION

This book is dedicated to my grandmother Birdie West, long since gone to the big bakery in the sky where she is no doubt teaching other children how to make a decent cake. Thanks, Grandmother, for taking time with me when I was a little kid and hung on your every word.

introduction

I still remember perfectly the day I gave up baking cakes from scratch. I'd invested a significant amount of time and energy in assembling the ingredients and then making and baking the layers for a friend's birthday cake. Upon removing it from the oven, however, I was dismayed to find that I'd created yet another "volcano" cake. You probably know the kind—it rises in the middle as if ready to erupt at any moment and may actually crack into pieces. A true disaster for any home baker.

"Why," I railed at the cake baking gods, "can't I make a simple cake as well as my grandmother did?"

I tried to ice my misshapen masterpiece, hoping to cover up the damage, only to discover, to my even greater frustration, that the frosting wouldn't stay on. It just kept sliding down the sides of the volcano like lava run amok. I had a sink full of pots, pans, bowls, and utensils, with nothing to show for my efforts but a cake not even its creator could love.

"This never happened when I was a kid and my grandmother kept a cake on the sideboard at all times," I muttered.

That's when I, like millions of Americans, succumbed to the lure of the mix. With mixes, I did get predictable results. The layers were flat and stackable, and the frosting stayed where it was supposed to. The only problem was that the taste and texture simply didn't measure up.

The taste of a "mix" cake is nothing like homemade. You have to know that the minute you put one in the oven. Where is that heavenly aroma of good butter and sugar, real vanilla, and fine chocolate? Any baker can tell you that the quality of the finished product depends on the quality of the ingredients from which it is made. When the product is a mix cake, the ingredients include too many chemicals—added, by the way, to increase the shelf life of the mix and for no other reason. And the texture of the cake, while certainly tender, never has the "crumb" that comes from home mixing. Box cakes have a deadening sameness of texture and only a hint of flavor difference, one from the other.

As a veteran seeker and innovator in the kitchen, I set out on a quest, determined to find a way to make cakes that were not only consistently symmetrical but also predictably tender and moist, with the flavor and aroma of fine fresh ingredients, and that didn't require large blocks of time spent in the kitchen, mixing, baking, and cleaning up.

I got lucky. The first piece of the puzzle came from behind the counter at a bakery shop. A pro told me he bakes every cake at 400° F and only uses shiny aluminum pans. Why? I asked. Cakes come up faster, cool down faster and the resulting crust and crumb are better. Layers are as disk-like as Frisbees. It also helps the professional keep his ovens cranking out cakes all day long. But that's another story. I took what he told me and applied the skills I've acquired as a professional cookbook writer and creator of recipes. Eureka! I found a system that works.

Great cakes depend on three basic elements: ingredients, technique, and equipment. The secret to baking great cakes in half the time is to use the best available ingredients; to combine them according to my simple but specific method, which cuts the mixing time by at least 20 percent; and to bake them in a particular kind of pan at a higher temperature that reduces baking time by 30 percent.

Cakes made from scratch contain only fresh ingredients— no preservatives and no chemicals. Here, you will learn a quick, efficient procedure for making cakes, and you'll learn how to bake successfully at a hotter temperature, which yields a superior product in less time.

With *Cakes From Scratch in Half the Time*, any home cook will soon be making cupcakes that bake in 10 minutes, layer cakes that bake in 15 minutes rather than 25 to 30, and tubes, loaves, and Bundts that bake in 35 to 45 minutes rather than an hour and a half or so. The results will be predictable, and the cook, in most instances, will be out of the kitchen in less than an hour.

It was not easy to master this technique. Trust me when I tell you that it took a lot of trial and error to perfect the technique you see here. And, like the last ground-breaking baking book I wrote, *Bread in Half the Time* (winner of the International Association of Culinary Professionals Best Cookbook of the Year award), the early trials focused on errors.

I can tell that a recipe isn't even worth trying after the first shot when the dog refuses to eat it and takes it out into the backyard and buries it. In 1991, the dogs salted the backyard with failed breads—read bricks. This year, the dirt flew as the dog buried failed cakes. When the archaeologists dig up my backyard in a thousand years and discover this cache of rock-hard, burned breads and cakes, they will surely believe it to be some sort of ancient, mysterious religious rite. They will be correct. Reaching cake nirvana took a lot of practice, a lot of praying, and a certain amount of cursing and gnashing of teeth. It also took a lot of refinement in the method.

But I believe you have before you a book that will help you make a great cake. And in half the time. After being hip-deep in cake batter for two years, I can still say that I love cake baking passionately, and I am now the one who says, when somebody invites me to a potluck, "Let me bring the cake."

I expect to get some flak over the method I'm proposing. Ten years ago, when Diana Butts and I first presented our ideas for baking breads, we were told that what we proposed was heresy. We had to change agents. It took us more than a year and a half to sell the idea. But that book was named the best cookbook of the year in America, and the method we developed is now fairly standard in cookbooks. Cuisinart's latest model food processor even has a "dough" button. Diana and I did that. We taught people how to make bread in a food processor. And now I'm going to teach you how to make great cakes in cheap pans and a hot oven.

Just last week, I made a Bûche de Noël that took less than an hour and a half for the whole, complicated process. Noel, the soon-to-be-six-year-old grandchild, said, "Gamma, I want a log just like this for my birthday." And Lily, Noel's twin sister, chimed in, "I want cupcakes. Barbie pink ones." "No problem," I answered. "Your wish is my command." For you see, now I get to be the cake-baking grandmother. And what a pleasure that is.

By making small but significant changes in technique, while always relying on the best ingredients and professional standard home equipment, I have evolved this new method for baking cakes quickly and easily. The resulting cake has a better crust and crumb and an excellent flavor, and—best of all—is easier to do than starting with a cake mix. Most importantly, once you learn this easy technique, you will find cake baking to be totally predictable. And in most cases, you'll be in and out of the kitchen in one hour or less.

I have updated classic recipes using this new, improved method, cutting the mixing time by at least 20 percent and the baking time by 30 percent. Cakes made famous by fine bakeries and fabulous hobby cooks can be yours. Your friends and family will swear you've been taking a pastry class. Best of all, you will never be puzzled by odd-looking, lumpy cakes or strange chemical tastes that come from mixes. Baking a cake will become as natural for you as it was for your grandmother.

And that's saying something.

—Linda West Eckhardt
Maplewood, New Jersey

The Three Keys to
GREAT CAKES

· Baking Method ·

· Mixing Technique ·

· Basic Ingredients ·

The order of this chapter may seem a bit odd at first. Don't the ingredients, after all, come before the mixing and baking? That may be true, but—except when it comes to dessert—I've never been a great advocate of saving the best for last, and it was unlocking the professional baking method that bakers had so long been hiding that provided the key to transforming my cake-baking life.

the baking method

It happened, as I said, in a bakery. I was standing at the counter when I saw the baker pulling out a rack of perfectly baked layers. I couldn't resist asking, "How do you do that? Why can't I do it too?"

"It's simple," he said, running a knife around one of the battered-looking pans he'd just taken from the oven and flipping out a luscious, caramel brown, perfectly uniform disk. "All you need is a good recipe, great ingredients, a shiny aluminum pan, and a four-hundred-degree oven."

Recipes and ingredients I knew about. It was the pans and the oven temperature that caught me totally by surprise. Weren't those cheap, shiny aluminum pans the ones we'd relegated to the back of the cupboard when we bought our new, nonstick, Teflon-coated, dark metal ones that seemed so much more—well—professional? And in my vast collection of cookbooks by professional bakers, cooking teachers, and inspired amateurs I'd never seen a single-layer cake recipe that called for a 400°F oven.

This was an opportunity too good to pass up. As I pressed him further, the baker went on to explain the reasons behind his method, and I discovered that there was, indeed, method in his apparent madness. Shiny aluminum pans conduct heat evenly, so that the layers come out uniform every time. And they cool down quickly, so that the cakes can be stacked and frosted sooner than if they'd had to sit waiting for their pans to cool before they could be turned out. The oven temperature—about 50° hotter than in conventional recipes—allows for more batches per day. The result, as required by the professional baker, is a quality product that can be replicated with predictable results in the quantities necessary for commercial establishments.

Of course, I was aware that commercial ovens are more finely calibrated, which means their temperatures are more reliable, than the average home oven. But any variation in temperature in the home oven can be accommodated easily if you have an independent oven thermometer—an inexpensive piece of equipment that is essential if you are going to be baking great cakes in half the time.

Look in the back of your cupboards. You may already have some shiny aluminum pans. If not, go out and get some. They're about the least expensive kind of pans you can buy. (See page 189 for mail-order sources.)

the mixing technique

The method in this book is essentially an updated version of the cake-mixing technique I learned all those years ago in home ec, and it's still the most efficient way to mix the batter for most cakes.

1. Gather all your ingredients on the countertop. Place the eggs, in their shells, in a bowl of hot tap water to take the chill off.

2. Turn the oven to 400°F to preheat. If the oven is under your stovetop, put the butter, in its wrapper, on the stovetop to soften. If not, put it in the microwave for about 15 seconds, just long enough to take the chill off without melting it. Prepare your pans according to the recipe directions.

3. In an electric stand mixer, begin beating the butter and sugar together. As the mixer is doing its work, measure the dry ingredients into a sifter or strainer and place it over a sheet of wax paper on one side of the mixer.

Measure the wet ingredients into a liquid measuring cup and place it on the other side of the mixer.

4. Break the warmed eggs into the butter/sugar mixture, incorporating each one before adding the next. Then, with the mixer still going, and starting with the dry ingredients, add the wet and dry ingredients alternately to the mixer, spooning in the flour a tablespoon at a time. As soon as all the ingredients are incorporated, stop mixing. The key is not to overmix, because the texture of your cake will suffer if you do.

That's it. You're now ready to turn the batter into the prepared pan or pans and bake. The entire mixing process should have taken you no more than 5 or 6 minutes. And for cleanup you'll have only measuring cups, spoons, one sifter, and one bowl.

If you're using a hand-held rather than a stand mixer, you'll have to do a bit more juggling, since you won't have two free hands, but the process remains the same, and the result will be the same as well.

the ingredients

Now we get to the basics. Start with the highest-quality ingredients appropriate for the task, and you'll be assured of an aromatic, well-textured, delicious result every time.

FLOUR

The main differences among types of flour derive from the kind of wheat used—hard or soft—and their protein content. Cake and pastry flours are made from soft wheat and are also the lowest in protein, at about 4 percent. As a result,

they absorb less moisture, which means they produce the tenderest cakes, pies, biscuits, and muffins. Softasilk, Swans Down, and White Lily are the brands of choice. I use White Lily whenever I can and have been known to smuggle back suitcases full of it from the South (See Mail-Order Sources, page 189).

Bread flour, which has to stand up to heavy kneading in order to develop its elasticity, is made from hard wheat and is also highest in protein, at about 14 percent. It is never used for making cakes unless they are leavened with yeast.

All-purpose flour, as its name implies, lies somewhere in the middle. It's made from a combination of hard and soft wheat and contains 10 to 11 percent protein. While all-purpose flour can, in theory, be used in any cake recipe, it won't yield as delicate a product as you'll get using cake flour. Choose all-purpose flour only when the cake includes fruits and nuts and, therefore, requires a sturdier structure. Pillsbury is the best all-purpose flour I know and is what I prefer.

You'll note that most recipes call for "sifted flour." If you're an absolute purist, sift the flour before you measure it. But for the rest of us, presume that the flour you bought has been sifted once (it has!) and go forth.

MEASURING FLOUR Dip, scoop, and level. That's the watchword for measuring flour. For greatest accuracy, fluff up the flour with a fork while it's still in the bag, then dip a dry measuring cup of the proper size into the bag and scoop out the flour. Don't jiggle or bang it on the counter. Just scrape a knife across the measuring cup to level the top, and then transfer the flour to a strainer or sifter. Never pack it into the cup. You could add a full ¼ cup too much by doing this, and the result would be a dry, lifeless cake.

All flour absorbs moisture from the air, which is why professional bakers measure it by weight rather than volume. For the home baker, however, volume is the standard method of measuring.

STORING FLOUR Flour has a shelf life of approximately 6 months, so don't buy more than you can use in that period of time. Store it in a dark place in an opaque, airtight container. Smell it before you use it. If it's bad, it will smell rancid. Take a good look. If it seems lumpy and clumped, it's absorbed a lot of moisture and you may have to add a few minutes to the baking time to allow the cake to dry. If, on the other hand, it seems dry as sawdust, your cake will probably be done in a few minutes less than is called for in the recipe. In either case, you'll be able to tell when you test it for doneness, either by inserting a toothpick in the center and seeing if it comes out clean, or by pressing the center of the cake with your finger to see if it springs back.

LIQUIDS

Milk is the liquid most commonly used in baking because it contains both calcium and fat, which provide structure for the cake. For the best taste and texture, use whole milk, which contains 4 percent fat. When you're already using butter, sugar, eggs, and flour, reducing the fat content by using 2 percent milk isn't going to make very much difference— except in the quality of the final product. Chocolate and some spice cakes sometimes call for buttermilk, which gives them a subtle tangy flavor. Powdered and canned milks have distinct flavors that adversely affect the flavor of the cake and are, therefore, not usually recommended.

For optimum results, pour the milk into a liquid measuring cup with a pouring lip and put it in the microwave for 15 to 20 seconds to take the chill off before using it in a recipe.

If the recipe calls for cream, it pays to read the label on the container. Pasteurized heavy cream has a higher butterfat content than so-called whipping cream and a better flavor than that of ultrapasteurized cream, and so it is the ultimate for cake baking and frostings. It's hard to find, however. You may have to make a trip to Whole Foods or another luxe grocer to find anything beyond so-called whipping cream. But it may be worth it to you. Pasteurized heavy cream doesn't have the shelf life of the ultra-pasteurized kind and is therefore fresher and more flavorful than its long-lived cousin.

Half and-half is just what it says—half milk and half cream. It won't whip, nor will it work as well as whole milk as the liquid in a cake batter. To recap, if the recipe calls for milk, use whole milk. If it calls for cream, use heavy cream. This is true whether you are using this or any other book of cake recipes.

BUTTER AND OTHER FATS

All of the recipes in this book call for unsalted (sometimes called sweet) butter. It's more fragile than salted butter— remember that, before the widespread use of refrigeration, salt was used to "cure" and preserve both butter and meat— so unsalted butter should either be kept frozen or used quickly after purchasing. If a recipe calls for shortening, use only pure vegetable shortening and don't try to substitute oil, which would impart a wet and greasy texture to the cake, and which won't work for greasing the pan. There are a few recipes that call for vegetable oil, but these are the exceptions and call for alternate mixing methods.

EGGS

Use large eggs for the recipes in this book. Using other sizes of eggs will throw off the balance of the formula. I prefer organic eggs because I think they have the best flavor.

The date on which the eggs were packed will give you a better sense of their freshness than the "best if used by" date. You can find the packing date by looking at the end of the carton. The "P" number tells you *where* they were packed. The three-digit number either preceding or following that indicates the specific day of the Julian calendar on which they were packed. The Julian calendar numbers the days of the year from 1 through 365, so, for example, eggs marked 365 would have been packed on New Year's Eve. The recipes in this book call for eggs to be at room temperature before they are combined with creamed fat and sugar. Cold eggs could harden the fat and curdle the batter, which might affect the texture of the finished cake. Always warm the eggs to 70°F, either by setting them out on the countertop for a half hour or so or, more simply, by submerging them in hot tap water while you assemble the rest of the ingredients for the cake.

SALT

I use kosher salt in all of these (and other) recipes. Table salt has too many additives and chemicals that throw off the flavor of the cake, and sea salt contains too much iodine to be used in baking.

SUGAR

Most cakes are made with granulated sugar. If a recipe calls for a combination of granulated and some other type of sugar—for example, confectioners' or brown sugar—don't try to substitute one for the other. Baking is a science that doesn't leave much room for changing the formula. When I need to use brown sugar, I almost always select dark brown sugar, but you can use whatever type suits you. Confectioners' sugar seems to be the worst for getting lumpy. It's always best to run it through the strainer before measuring it. Almost always, you'll find clumps to throw away.

BAKING POWDER

All baking powder sold in the United States is now "double acting." It's used as a leavening agent, and the first rising action occurs when you add the liquid to the batter. The second action occurs once the cake is exposed to the heat of the oven. The cake must go into the oven promptly after it's mixed in order to derive the benefit of both actions.

Baking powder remains active for about a year. Check the expiration date, and always store it tightly covered in a dark cabinet.

BAKING SODA

Not all recipes require both baking powder and baking soda. Those that do are generally chocolate cakes or others that include an acid, such as buttermilk, lemon juice, or vinegar. Most recipes in this book call for Dutch process cocoa, which has been alkalized and demands baking soda to foment the rising action. In these recipes the leavening occurs when the baking soda and the acid combine to form carbon dioxide gas, which raises the batter. You didn't know you were making your own kitchen combustibles, did you? Cake baking is science, and if you understand the principles, you are halfway home.

FAT FOR THE PAN

Commonly known in the trade as release agents, these are simply anything that keeps the cake from sticking to the pan. Most traditional cake recipes (other than angel food cakes, which require a dry pan) call for greasing the pan with butter or vegetable shortening, dusting it with flour, shaking out the excess, and sometimes even lining the bottom with parchment or wax paper. All of that is time-consuming and, luckily, no longer necessary.

I strongly suggest that you do as I've done and discover the joy of using Baker's Joy or another brand of quick-release spray that combines fat and flour. One quick spray and your pan is prepared! Don't try this with aerosol cans of vegetable or olive oil, though. They will give the cake a sticky finish that won't release from the pan. And don't use oil; the batter will slide down rather than climbing up the sides of the pan.

If you must, prepare the pans the old-fashioned way. Just be sure not to overdo either the shortening or the flour, and do be sure to thoroughly grease every bit of the bottom and sides and into all the corners. After you've done this a few times, you might see the wisdom of trying Baker's Joy!

If you're making a chocolate cake, substituting unsweetened cocoa powder for flour after greasing or spraying the pan will intensify the flavor and give the crust a nice rustic look.

CHOCOLATE AND COCOA

Chocolate is made by roasting and processing cocoa beans in various ways, much as coffee is made from coffee beans. Unsweetened baking chocolate results from beans that have been roasted, ground to a thick paste, and dried with all the chocolate liqueur and cocoa butter intact. Sugar is added to the paste in various quantities to create anything from bittersweet to pale "milk" chocolate. Removing some of the cocoa butter and drying the paste creates cocoa powder. Add sugar to the powder and you've created an "instant" hot cocoa mix.

Buying the finest-quality chocolate available is the first key to baking the best-quality cake. If you're working with cocoa, look for Dutch process. For bar chocolate, French Valrhona is almost universally considered the *ne plus ultra*. It's exceptional in every respect, including price, but other fine chocolates are also widely available including Dutch Droste, Swiss Lindt, French Tobler, and American Ghirardelli or Guittard. (See page 189 for mail-order sources.)

The second key to working successfully with chocolate is to be sure you're using the right one for your recipe. The various kinds of chocolate can't be substituted one for the other without unexpected and sometimes disastrous results.

Unsweetened chocolate has no sugar added, and if you tried to eat it, you wouldn't be happy. It's sold in the baking section of supermarkets as baking chocolate and is usually subdivided into paper-wrapped 1-ounce squares.

Bittersweet or semisweet chocolate has some sugar added, and this is where investing in quality will stand you in good stead. Any of the brands mentioned earlier will produce a better-tasting cake than the ones to be found in the baking aisle.

Milk chocolate is paler and less flavorful than bittersweet or semisweet and isn't recommended for baking.

Separating the cocoa butter from the chocolate liqueur and mixing it with sugar and powdered milk makes white chocolate. It varies widely in quality, and poor-quality white chocolate can be both tasteless and unpleasant in texture. A good confectionary is the place to find the best.

If you must make a chocolate cake right now and don't have the right kind of chocolate for your recipe, here are a few substitutions you can use.

- 1 ounce unsweetened chocolate = 3 tablespoons unsweetened cocoa powder + 1 tablespoon sugar
- 1 ounce semisweet chocolate = ½ ounce unsweetened chocolate + 1 tablespoon sugar
- 6 ounces semisweet chocolate = 6 tablespoons unsweetened cocoa powder + 7 tablespoons sugar + ¼ cup vegetable shortening

STORING CHOCOLATE All chocolate should be stored in a cool, dark place. Exposing it to rapid changes in temperature and/or humidity can cause a whitish "bloom" to form on the surface, although for baking the bloom will not affect the quality of the chocolate or the finished product.

WORKING WITH CHOCOLATE Chop chocolate with a sharp knife or in a food processor using the "pulse" function so that you don't overheat and inadvertently melt it.

Grate chocolate on a box grater, in a food processor, or best of all, using a new gadget called a Microplane that creates perfect shards to be used as decoration or combined with a batter.

Melt chocolate in a microwave or in a double boiler over hot, not boiling, water. If you use the microwave, the chocolate won't actually appear to have melted. Start by setting the time at 30 seconds and test by pressing it with a skewer or a fork to determine when it's done. Two 1-ounce squares of unsweetened chocolate will melt in about 1 minute. Two ounces of semisweet or 4 ounces of milk chocolate will melt in about 1½ minutes.

FRUITS AND VEGETABLES

Several of the recipes in this book call for fresh fruits or vegetables. As always, buying the freshest and best will yield the tastiest result.

Fresh zests and juices will provide better flavor than even the best extracts. Use a zester or Microplane to shred the zest and a reamer to extract the juice. Putting a lemon or orange in the microwave for 30 seconds before zesting and/ or juicing will boost the flavor even more.

NUTS

Many of the recipes call for a specific kind of nut, including walnuts, pecans, hazelnuts, almonds, and peanuts. With the exception of peanuts, it's almost always possible to substitute one variety for another.

Buy the best quality you can find, and know that the less breakage they've been subjected to before you buy them, the more flavor they will yield. Buy them either whole or halved, double-wrap them, and store them in the freezer. Shopping in a store that has a high turnover will further assure their freshness.

ROASTING NUTS Roasting nuts brings out their aroma and flavor. Spread them in a single layer on a Silpat-lined or parchment-lined baking sheet and put them in a 350°F oven for no more than 5 to 8 minutes, just until they begin to brown and give off a heavenly, nutty aroma. Immediately transfer them to a cool container to stop the cooking process. If you burn them, don't try to use them. Just start over. This is something you'll learn from truly bitter experience.

VANILLA EXTRACT

I'm happy to report that it turns out that artificial vanilla extract yields as much flavor as the so-called pure vanilla extract, and it's a whole lot cheaper. Steeping chopped vanilla beans in an alcohol-and-water solution makes pure vanilla extract. Imitation vanilla extract is made from vanillin, a product extracted from conifer wood pulp that has been chemically rinsed. But never mind. Chris Kimball and the true testers at America's Test Kitchen did a double-blind study and found that, when used in baking, artificial vanilla extract yielded as satisfying a vanilla hit as the genuine article. So save yourself a few bucks. Buy the artificial kind.

Those of you who visit Mexico have an opportunity to buy the pluperfect, best-flavored vanilla made on earth. Sold in big fifth-sized whiskey-style bottles, vanilla extract from Mexico has such a punched-up flavor that you will have to be parsimonious with its use, but once you try it, you'll want it from then on. It's a flavor hit like no other. Be warned, however, that some Mexican vanilla contains coumarin, which is toxic. You can buy FDA-approved, coumarin-free vanilla from Nutrition Lifestyles (see Mail-Order Sources, page 189). They sell two brands by mail order, both of which are FDA approved, guaranteed pure and free of coumarin.

cake-speak

For those who want all the nitty-gritty details or, perhaps, who have less experience using baking recipes, we offer the following decoding of the mysterious language of cake bakers.

Every craft has its jargon or vernacular, a kind of shorthand that communicates perfectly to initiates into the craft, but often seems completely mysterious to the uninitiated. Cake bakers have cake-speak. Listed here are common cake-speak phrases found in this and other baking books, followed by an explanation so that you'll know what the heck you're reading about and what you are being instructed to do.

Making cake batter involves combining ingredients in a specific order and with specific techniques so that not only are the ingredients well mixed, but enough air is admitted to the finished batter so that when it goes into the oven, to be introduced to that blast of hot air, it can rise perfectly to yield a cake that is both moist and tender, with a fine, even crumb.

One of the most common problems for today's cake bakers is that most cut their teeth using cake mixes, which have a completely different method. It's not that making a cake from scratch is harder, or takes longer. On the contrary, once you get the hang of it, you will wonder why you ever tolerated cake mixes, with their inevitable chemical aroma and taste.

"Cream the butter and sugar." This is shorthand for mixing the butter and sugar in a stand mixer until the two elements are one and the mixture appears light and fluffy. If you rub a little of the creamed mixture between your fingers, you'll find that the sugar is almost dissolved. This can take up to 3 minutes to do properly.

"Add the eggs, one at a time." Simply break the eggs into the mixer, one at a time, after the butter and sugar are creamed, with the motor running. Let the mixer run while you go to the next step. Go ahead and sift the flour while the mixer runs.

"Sift . . ." All you're doing here is aerating the flour and other dry ingredients together. You don't have to own a formal sifter like the one your mother used. I just dump all the dry ingredients into a sieve or colander, then hold it about 12 inches above a piece of wax paper and shake it so the ingredients fall to the paper, like flakes of snow. Knock the sieve against the palm of your other hand to increase the flow.

"Add the dry and wet ingredients alternately to the butter mixture . . ." Just make a rough approximation and add a spoon or two of the flour mixture, then a sip of milk, then a spoon or so of the flour, a sip of milk, and so on. Before you know it, the mixture will be perfect, all the ingredients will be incorporated, and the mixture will look even in color and texture. Stop the mixer. Do *not* continue to mix for 2 minutes (as all cake mix instructions say), or you will deflate the batter.

"Scrape . . ." Depending on the type of stand mixer you use, you may need to stop the machine and scrape down the sides of the bowl using a rubber spatula. I have an old-fashioned stand mixer with two bowls—a big one and a little one—and

I can easily scrape down the sides while the motor is running. Don't try that with a Kitchenaid-type mixer, though, or you're likely to send the spatula flying through the air—in pieces. The point here is that batter may stick to the sides of the bowl and need to be reincorporated into the rest of the batter. Use your own two good eyes, and scrape as needed.

"Whisk in . . ." This is usually the last step and implies that you're not using the stand mixer but a balloon whisk to incorporate air as well as two or more ingredients at the very end. Often you're instructed to do this because the electric mixer might overdo the process and deflate the batter.

"Fold in . . ." When making batter, you will not only mix the ingredients but also incorporate air. At the end of the process, you may be asked to lightly add one last ingredient. This could be beaten egg whites or nuts or fruits. Whatever it is, you don't want to lose the air you've beaten into the batter, so you simply sprinkle the ingredient over the top and, using a rubber spatula or wooden spoon, incorporate it by plunging the spatula into the batter and making a bottom-to-top loop. Turn the bowl with your hand and do it again. Before you know it, that final ingredient will be mixed and the batter will be as full of air as it was to start with. Should you try to fold ingredients in using the stand mixer, you would undoubtedly deflate the batter and get a cake that was dense and coarse rather than one lighter than the proverbial feather.

"Pour the batter . . ." Most cake batter is liquid enough to pour easily into the prepared cake pan. Run a rubber spatula around the edges of the bowl to get every last bit of batter into the pan, and pass the spatula over the top to smooth it. Now scoot the cake into the preheated oven on the middle rack, close the door, set the timer, and stand back.

"Test with a wooden pick." When a cake is baked thoroughly, several things happen. The hot blast of air causes the chemicals in the batter to expand. Think of it as being like blowing a bubble with a piece of bubble gum. That's exactly what happens to the cake batter—whether the leavening is baking powder for sweet milk cakes, baking soda for buttermilk, or just plain beaten egg whites, you'll see first that the top is golden or dark brown. The center should be standing up slightly, and a wooden pick or toothpick inserted into the center should not have a speck of wet cake batter on it. If there is batter, just shove the cake back into the oven for 5 minutes or so. Experienced cake bakers can also judge doneness by touching the top of the cake with a finger. If the indention remains, the cake is not done. The fast cooking method used in this book yields a glorious full brown crust that may startle you the first time you see it. Do not worry. It's not going to burn, because you're going to take it out of the oven at the first moment you can, once the cake is baked.

"To frost . . ." or not to frost. It's always a question with cake. Although I have appended many varieties of frosting to the recipes, feel free to mix and match them or to send your cake into the world with nothing more than a dusting of confectioners' sugar. Suit yourself. See the index for a cross reference to all the frostings in the book.

the right stuff

THE RIGHT EQUIPMENT

The first thing you need to do when you enter the kitchen is crank the oven up to 400°F. And don't put that cake into the oven until the temperature is reached. I never trust the oven thermostat. It is common for them to be off by as much as 50°. In other words, your oven could actually be 350° or 450°F, and I daresay you don't have the skills that our grand-mothers had when they could simply put their hand into a hot oven and tell you when it was ready.

An independent oven thermometer is a must for all bakers. You can pick one up at the grocery store and hang it on the middle shelf of the oven. It won't last too long. Expect the heat to soften the metal until it will barely stand in place. A better solution is to get a thermometer on a magnet that you can affix to the inside of the oven door.

A heavy-duty stand mixer. Besides the gold standard, Kitchenaid, there are a number of equally good mixers on the market. For this book, I actually used an old-fashioned Hamilton Beach, the kind with two bowls, a big and a little one, and twin beaters. At 300 watts of power, and for a cost of less than $70, I found it quite sufficient for the job. Having two bowls makes switching from egg whites to egg yolks easy. If you own a Kitchenaid, may I suggest you buy yourself an extra bowl? Otherwise, switching back and forth makes you crazy. One last word of advice: You don't have to wash the bowl you just beat the egg whites in if you've transferred them and are now ready to beat the yolks. A little beaten egg white does no harm whatsoever to egg yolks at work. If you're using a Kitchenaid, remember that the paddle is used for creaming butter and sugar and for mixing batters, and the balloon whip is used for beating egg whites or cream. Use only the highest settings for beating egg whites or whipping cream. For most tasks, set it somewhere in the middle, say on speed 4.

A food processor is useful for chopping nuts, grating chocolate or carrots, and breaking down ingredients you want to include in the cake. Not a day goes by that I don't use my Kitchenaid food processor.

A microwave is always handy for melting chocolate and butter. It's also great for warming up ingredients. The microwave is not suitable for baking cakes, because it does not cook by radiant heat and will not brown or caramelize the food properly. If you don't have a microwave, don't sweat it. Anything that can be done in a microwave can be done on the stove; it just may not be quite as handy. Melt chocolate in a double boiler over hot but not boiling water. Melt butter over low heat. Warm liquids just until tiny bubbles form on the edge of the pan.

Baking pans. This trade secret comes to you by way of Greg Skipper, who has been supplying bakers from amateurs to America's finest boutique bakeries with pans for 15 years. His Web site is invaluable (see Mail-Order Sources, page 189). Greg's shiny, commercial-grade aluminum baking pans are spun, not punched, and have the following advantages that professional bakers demand:

- Aluminum pans bake cakes in 30 percent less time than pans made from other materials.
- They transfer heat quickly and cool quickly so that cakes rise evenly and brown evenly.
- Using the proper pans, you'll get no more "volcano" layers that rise up in the middle like Vesuvius.
- You'll get no more hot spots.
- They conduct heat better than stainless steel pans, which are unreliable heat conductors. Steel gets too hot and will cause the cake's outside to darken and crack, while the center never gets done.
- They are also superior to dark coated pans (so-called nonstick finishes), which attract too much heat and cause cakes to overbrown.
- Aluminum pans that are spun (like blowing glass) have perfectly straight sides, for that architectural look in a cake.
- They are dishwasher safe.

- They last a lifetime.
- They may darken because aluminum will react with acidic foods, but can easily be restored by a boiling water bath in which a spoon full of cream of tartar has been added.
- They are economical. An 8-inch round cake pan costs about six bucks. Need I say more?
- A quick spritz with a release agent (like Baker's Joy) will make it possible to make cakes all day long that fall right out of the pan. Nothing sticks.

Check out Greg's Web site and get out your credit card. If you're serious about cake baking, you need to order yourself a range of pans. I buy most all of mine from this source.

OTHER USEFUL GEAR

What about a sifter? I got rid of the triple sifter my high school home ec teacher made me buy a long time ago. Now I just use an Ikea plastic colander. I dump the dry ingredients in and shake it over a piece of wax paper, using the heel of my hand to rap the edge of the colander to hasten the flour's passage to the paper. The idea behind sifting is to aerate the flour. A strainer, colander, sieve, or sifter all do the job quite adequately. Just use what's on hand.

Measuring cups and spoons. Nested dry measures up to 1 cup plus a glass measure with a lip that goes up to 2 cups plus measuring spoons are all you need. Baking is a science, and you can't monkey around with the volume of ingredients. Eyeball the liquids by holding the glass measure up to eye level so you can see. Rake off excess dry ingredients by passing a knife blade across the top of the measuring cup and spoons. This will make your life a whole lot smoother. The best surprise in baking is no surprise, and accurate measurement is mandatory.

Rubber spatulas help with all the scraping and pouring you'll be doing. The new generation of spatulas are heat resistant and don't seem to take up guck from the dishwasher as the old ones did.

Wooden spoons are really useful for hand-mixing one-bowl cakes.

Silpat is a new gizmo from France (what would we do without the French for great culinary inventions?) that makes baking a jelly roll a dream. Simply slap this silicone-impregnated cloth in the bottom of the baking pan, pour the batter over it, and bake away. There's no need to grease or spray the pan. The cake just peels right off. A quick wipe of the Silpat is all that's needed to clean it. This tool is a boon to cake bakers.

The Microplane is the best kitchen tool to come down the pike in many a year. Sold as a carpenter's rasp for two generations, it made its way to the kitchen when an enterprising heir to a small company discovered how useful the rasp was for grating chocolate, nutmeg, lemon, cinnamon, and cheese. You name it, the Microplane will grate it. When you're done, just pop it into the dishwasher. It's really the greatest.

Papers and wraps are useful when baking cakes. I generally sift flour mixtures onto wax paper because then I can just pick up the paper, form it into a kind of funnel, and slide every last bit onto the cake batter. I use shiny aluminum foil to reflect the heat back when I'm making loaf cakes. In that case, a quick spritz of Baker's Joy on the shiny side of the foil will prevent the cake from sticking to the foil as it rises in the oven and will prevent overbrowning. I use plastic wrap to seal loaf cakes and other cake layers I might want to freeze for a few days. I also press plastic wrap against the surface of frostings and custards that are cooling in the refrigerator. Parchment paper can be used to roll jelly rolls, to line pans, and for many other chores where you don't want something to stick and you need a paper product that can withstand both heat and moisture.

A cake bell is simply a glass or plastic cover to protect the cake from dry air or air that is too moist.

A WORD ABOUT OVENS

In my kitchen I have a Chambers gas range and a Kitchenaid electric wall oven that offers both convection and radiant heat. For most cakes, I use the convection feature at 400°F. However, for loaves and Bundt cakes, I find it best to turn the convection off, because it tends to brown the surface too fast.

I actually believe that the difference between gas and electric is more significant than that between convection and not. A gas oven switches off and on to maintain the heat, often sending a blast of hot air into the oven in the middle of baking, whereas an electric coil seems to radiate a more even wave of heat. I prefer electric ovens.

The most significant thing to know about using an oven is that every time you open the door during the baking cycle, you let in a blast of cold air, which not only screws up the timing of the recipe, but also offers the chance for the cake to fall. I mean, wouldn't you shrink in the face of a blast of cold air? *Never open the oven door until the minimum baking time has elapsed*, except with loaves, where you have to whisk off the foil after 25 minutes of cooking. Do not tarry. Get that foil off and close the oven promptly and gently.

When I was a kid, my cake-baking grandmother even warned me against running across the kitchen floor because it might makes the cake fall. This is no joke. If you are baking in an oven on an unstable floor (say in an RV or a camp house), don't let the kids come romping across the kitchen floor or the cake might fall, and wouldn't that be awful?

ten easiest cakes for beginners to make

If you are new to baking and want to just dip your toe into the cake-baking stream, here are the easiest cakes in the book:

- a little plain cake with caramel pecan icing (page 33)

- rhoda berman's banana sour cream cake with lemon glaze (page 80)

- black bottom cupcakes (page 119)

- chocolate sauerkraut sheet cake (page 134)

- classic jelly roll (page 146)

- lazy daisy sheet cake with easy icing (page 128)

- mocha fudge chip pudding cake (page 93)

- traditional 1-2-3-4 cake with lemon filling and frosting (page 35)

- tunnel of fudge cake (page 56)

- wellesley fudge cupcakes (page 120)

1

Classic Layer
CAKES

Say "cake" to most people, and these cakes are what spring to mind. A wedge of two or three layers nestled in clouds of yummy frosting. Whether it be chocolate, coconut, butter, or vanilla, a layer cake is, to most of us, the quintessential item. With a moist, sweet crumb and a crisp, golden exterior, these cakes lend themselves to our new, warp-speed baking methods best of all. Use shiny aluminum baking pans, a 400°F oven, and my everything-old-is-new-again technique, and in 15 or 20 minutes you'll have layers so uniform you can sail them across the room like a Frisbee if you wish. No more Mount Vesuvius layers, no heaving tops you have to saw off; these layers will be so flat-topped they will stack as neatly as flapjacks.

Layer cakes have several distinct features. Most of them are so-called butter cakes. Soft butter or shortening is beaten or "creamed" with sugar until the mixture looks lighter in color as air bubbles are beginning to form. Keep your stand mixer set on medium speed in order to create a fine, even mesh of these fragile air cells. Then, along with the liquids and cake flour, baking powder or soda is added later to give the final boost when the cake lands in that blast of hot air in the oven.

You may have to unlearn what you learned using cake mixes. Remember how cake mix directions say to "beat for 2 minutes" after combining the ingredients? Making a scratch cake is actually easier and quicker than that. After you have creamed the butter and sugar and added the eggs one at a time, you add the liquid and the flour mixture alternately, in about four additions, starting and ending with the flour. The moment the mixture is blended, *stop*. If you overbeat this batter, you will get a dense, grainy cake because you will have beaten the air *out* of the batter. Overbeat it and you're likely to get something more like a kitchen sponge than a cake.

Old-time cooks like our grandmothers, who made cakes every week, could whip up a perfect cake with nothing more than a big bowl, a wooden spoon, and a wood stove. We may not have their skills with building fires, nor the muscles to make a cake by hand, but my goal here is to teach you to make a cake as light, as moist, and as tender as your grand-mother's. The first thing to know is that our so-called kitchen helpers, like stand mixers and convection ovens, work like a charm but must be treated with respect. Do not overbeat cake batter. Do not overbake the cake.

Sometimes, the old ways are the best. So don't be intimi-dated. Scratch layer cakes come together quicker than mak-ing a trip to the store for a mix or special ingredients.

These cakes get you in and out of the kitchen in under an hour. Whether you want a traditional 8- or 9-inch two- or three-layer cake or a special 6-inch cake to take for a house gift, they're all here. And I'll promise you one thing: Master the layer cake and you'll never consider using a cake mix again.

Cut into one of these beauties. Let the perfume work up your nose. Then tell me that the incessant chemical hit you get from cake mixes can compare. There's no contest. This is home baking at its best.

classic yellow cake

Cake mixes strive to be as good as this, but they simply can't compare. This cake is mellow, tender, and radiant with flavor. It goes together quickly, and it bakes into a gorgeous, golden brown cake that really doesn't need any finish at all. Dust it with confectioners' sugar, smear it with jam, top it with whipped cream. A sprinkling of berries, and it's pluperfect cake.

baker's tip

Sold your flour sifter at a garage sale for fifty cents? Dump the measured dry ingredients into a strainer, and tap the strainer against the heel of your hand over a piece of wax paper. Now your ingredients are perfectly sifted and sitting in a floury mountain at your right hand, waiting to be added to the mixer.

3 large eggs

2 cups sifted cake flour

2 teaspoons baking powder

½ teaspoon salt

½ cup (1 stick) soft, unsalted butter

1 cup sugar

2 teaspoons vanilla extract

¾ cup milk

1. PREPARE TO BAKE. Arrange the rack in the middle of the oven and preheat it to 400°F. Spritz two 8- or 9-inch shiny round aluminum cake pans or one 13-by-9-inch pan with Baker's Joy. Place the unbroken eggs in a bowl of hot tap water.

2. MAKE THE BATTER. Sift the flour, baking powder, and salt onto a sheet of wax paper. Cream the butter and sugar in a stand mixer until pale and fluffy, about 3 minutes. Beat in the eggs, one at a time, then the vanilla. Beat until thoroughly mixed, about 5 minutes. Spoon in the flour mixture alternately with the milk, in about 4 batches, starting with the flour. Mix just until the batter is smooth.

3. BAKE THE CAKE. Transfer the batter to the prepared pans. Bake until the cake begins to pull away from the sides and a wooden pick comes out clean, 15 to 20 minutes. Cool for 5 minutes in the pan on the rack, and then flip the layers out onto the rack to cool.

4. FINISH THE CAKE. Here's an easy frosting idea. All you need is a pint of perfect berries (any kind—strawberries, raspberries, blackberries, blueberries, or marionberries) and a half-pint of whipping cream. While the cake cools on the rack, beat the cream with 1 tablespoon sugar and ¼ teaspoon vanilla extract to soft peaks. Transfer one cake layer to a cake plate and add half of the whipped cream. Arrange some of the fresh berries in the cream. Top with the second layer and repeat, frosting the tops and sides with whipped cream and topping with the remaining berries.

lady baltimore white cake

Here's a white cake that managed to get an entire novel written about itself. The book, by Owen Wister, came out in 1906 and celebrated the magical powers of the famous Lady. A light, airy, three-layer confection bound with a cloudlike frosting studded with pecans, raisins, and figs and then kicked up with a jolt of bourbon, it's good enough for a small wedding. One day, when I was making this cake, I ran out of sugar and made a happy discovery. Brown sugar makes a fabulous icing—rustic, caramel colored, and actually more interesting than the original made with white sugar. Now I choose brown sugar more often than white. I don't think Lady Baltimore would mind.

baker's tip 〉 Although the original process was terribly convoluted, I've streamlined it so that you can be in and out of the kitchen in less than an hour. By switching around some of the traditional method, and baking in shiny aluminum pans, you'll get perfect disks that stack effortlessly.

8 large egg whites

1 cup (2 sticks) soft, unsalted butter

2 cups sugar

3½ cups sifted cake flour

1 tablespoon plus 1 teaspoon baking powder

¼ teaspoon salt

1 cup milk

2 teaspoons vanilla extract

1. PREPARE TO BAKE. Arrange the rack in the middle of the oven and preheat it to 400°F. Spritz three 8-inch shiny round aluminum cake pans with Baker's Joy. Place 8 unbroken eggs in a bowl of hot tap water for 5 minutes before separating.

2. MAKE THE BATTER. Separate the eggs (you will not need the yolks), and beat the whites in a large bowl until stiff, then transfer them to a second bowl. Cream the butter and sugar in the mixer until fluffy. Sift the flour, baking powder, and salt onto a piece of wax paper. Combine the milk and vanilla in a liquid measure. Spoon one third of the flour and half of the milk into the butter mixture, then spoon in one third of the flour, the remaining milk, and the remaining flour, beating constantly.

Fold the batter by hand into the beaten egg whites. Divide among the prepared pans.

3. BAKE THE CAKE. Bake until the cake is golden and pulls away from the sides of the pans, 15 to 20 minutes. Cool the layers in the pans on a rack for 5 minutes, then flip them out and cool on the rack. Place one layer on a cake stand lined with a doily.

LADY BALTIMORE'S FROSTING

2 cups sugar

¼ cup water

4 large egg whites

⅛ teaspoon salt

1 cup chopped pecans

½ cup golden raisins

6 dried figs, chopped

1 teaspoon vanilla extract

½ teaspoon almond extract

1 tablespoon bourbon or brandy

4. MAKE THE FROSTING. While the cake cools, combine the sugar and water in a small, heavy pan with a lip (such as Le Creuset) and bring it to a boil. Cook for 5 minutes. Meanwhile, beat the egg whites with the salt until frothy, then pour in the hot syrup in a thin stream. Keep beating at high speed until the frosting forms stiff peaks. Fold in the nuts, raisins, figs, vanilla and almond extracts, and bourbon. Scoop about 1 cup of the frosting onto the first layer. Spread with an offset spatula, top with the second layer, and repeat until you reach the top of the cake. Finish by frosting the sides of the cake. Serve warm or cool.

toasted triple coconut layer cake

If you love coconut, and you crave a tall, luscious slice of three-layer cake, this one's for you. Not only does it have coconut in the frosting, it has cream of coconut and coconut extract to ramp up the coconut flavor. If you prefer a lily-white cake, don't toast the coconut, but for maximum nutty, sweet flavor, by all means try it toasted.

baker's tip

Open the cream of coconut with a can opener, then stir to mix it before measuring. It may have separated. To add a sweet, crunchy note, drain some crushed pineapple and fold it into the frosting between the layers.

4 large eggs

½ teaspoon salt

½ cup (1 stick) soft, unsalted butter

1¾ cups sugar

1 cup canned sweetened cream of coconut (such as Coco Lopez)

½ teaspoon vanilla extract

½ teaspoon coconut extract

2¾ cups sifted cake flour

1 teaspoon baking powder

½ teaspoon baking soda

1 cup buttermilk

1. PREPARE TO BAKE. Arrange the rack in the middle of the oven and preheat it to 400°F. Spritz three 8-inch shiny round aluminum cake pans with Baker's Joy. Place the unbroken eggs in a bowl of hot tap water for 5 minutes before separating. Separate the eggs, placing the whites in a large mixer bowl. Beat the egg whites with a pinch of the salt until stiff but not dry. Transfer whites to another bowl and reserve.

2. MAKE THE BATTER. Cream the butter, sugar, and cream of coconut in a stand mixer until fluffy. Add the egg yolks, one at a time, and the vanilla and coconut extracts and beat on low speed. Meanwhile, sift the flour, baking powder, baking soda, and remaining salt onto a piece of wax paper. Then, with the mixer running at low speed, add the flour mixture and buttermilk to the egg mixture in thirds, alternately, until just combined. Fold in the egg whites by hand.

3. BAKE THE CAKE. Divide the batter among the prepared pans and bake until a wooden pick comes out clean, 15 to 20 minutes. Cool in the pans on a rack for 5 minutes, then flip the layers out onto the rack to cool.

continued

COCONUT FROSTING

16 ounces soft cream cheese

½ cup (1 stick) soft, unsalted butter

¼ cup canned sweetened
cream of coconut

1 teaspoon coconut extract

2 cups sifted confectioners' sugar

Pinch of salt

1 (10-ounce) package sweetened,
flaked coconut

4. MAKE THE FROSTING. Wash out the mixer bowl, then combine the cream cheese, butter, cream of coconut, and coconut extract in the bowl and beat on high speed until light and fluffy. Add the confectioners' sugar and salt and beat until light. Refrigerate while the cake cools. Toast the coconut by spreading it one layer deep on a baking sheet and toasting it until golden in a 400°F oven for about 4 minutes, stirring after 2 minutes.

5. FINISH THE CAKE. Place the bottom layer on a cake stand and add a generous dollop of frosting. Using an offset spatula, spread the frosting, then add a handful of toasted coconut and sprinkle evenly. Repeat with the second and third layers, adding a couple of toothpicks to each layer to secure it. Finally, frost the sides of the cake, and press the remaining toasted coconut onto the sides and top of the cake. Store under a cake bell.

a little plain cake with caramel pecan icing

If you went to your grandmother's house for visits, chances are this is what she meant when she said she had a "little plain cake." The cake is moist, tender, and sweet. You can finish it in a number of ways. We love our grandmama's easy Caramel Pecan Icing, but you could substitute whipped cream—maybe with sliced bananas.

baker's tip

Make the icing while the cake bakes. Let the layers cool on a rack for 15 minutes or so before you start stacking and icing them. Use an offset spatula for best results. Finish with pecan halves if you have them. Serve cut into wedges with a scoop of vanilla ice cream.

4 large eggs

1 cup (2 sticks) soft, unsalted butter

2 cups sugar

3 cups sifted cake flour

1 tablespoon baking powder

½ teaspoon salt

1 cup milk

2 teaspoons vanilla extract

1. PREPARE TO BAKE. Arrange the rack in the middle of the oven and preheat it to 400°F. Spritz three 8- or 9-inch shiny round aluminum cake pans with Baker's Joy. Place the unbroken eggs in a bowl of hot tap water.

2. MAKE THE BATTER. Cream the butter and sugar in a stand mixer until pale and fluffy. Add the eggs, one at a time, and continue beating. Sift the flour, baking powder, and salt onto a piece of wax paper. Combine the milk and vanilla in a liquid measure. Add to the butter mixture in thirds alternately with the milk mixture, beating just until the mixture is smooth.

3. BAKE THE CAKE. Transfer to the prepared pans. Bake until a wooden pick comes out clean, 15 to 20 minutes, then cool in the pans on a rack for 5 minutes. Run a knife blade around each layer, and flip them out onto the rack to cool for about 15 minutes.

continued

CARAMEL PECAN ICING
½ cup (1 stick) unsalted butter
2 cups firmly packed dark brown sugar
½ cup milk
½ teaspoon salt
3 cups sifted confectioners' sugar

1 cup pecan halves

4. MAKE THE ICING. While the cake is baking, melt the butter in a heavy-bottomed medium saucepan, and then add the brown sugar, milk, and salt, stirring to remove any lumps. Bring to a good, hard boil, then turn off the heat. Sift the confectioners' sugar into the mixture, stirring with a wooden spoon. Place a piece of plastic wrap down against the icing. Set it aside until the cake layers have cooled. Add a little milk if the icing seems too thick to spread.

5. FINISH THE CAKE. Transfer one layer to a cake plate. Spread about one third of the icing on top. Add the second layer and repeat, securing the layer with tooth-picks as needed. Add the third layer, and then use all the icing, covering the top and sides with an offset spatula. Finish the top with pecan halves arranged around the outer perimeter. Store under a cake bell.

traditional 1-2-3-4 cake with lemon filling and frosting

Originating in the nineteenth century, this cake still holds up today. The main ingredients are easy to remember: 1 cup butter, 2 cups sugar, 3 cups flour, and 4 eggs. You'll note that the process for making this cake is easier than the traditional method involving creaming the butter and sugar. Simply dump the ingredients into the mixing bowl, one at a time, and quick as a wink, you're ready to bake.

baker's tip

Timing is everything here. While the cake is baking, make the lemon curd. Use a heavy pan, take care to stir it constantly, and you can forget about a double boiler. Then, while the layers cool, make the frosting. Now, to orchestrate your masterpiece, transfer the first layer to a cake plate, slather it with curd, top it with the final layer(s), and finish the whole thing with frosting.

4 large eggs

3 cups sifted cake flour

1 tablespoon baking powder

½ teaspoon salt

1 cup (2 sticks) soft, unsalted butter

2 cups sugar

1 teaspoon vanilla extract

1 cup milk

1. PREPARE TO BAKE. Arrange the rack in the middle of the oven and preheat it to 400°F. Spritz two 8-inch or three 6-inch shiny round aluminum cake pans with Baker's Joy. Place the unbroken eggs into a bowl of hot tap water.

2. MAKE THE BATTER. Sift the flour, baking powder, and salt into the bowl of a stand mixer, then, with the mixer running, pinch off pieces of butter and add them one at a time. Add the sugar, a tablespoon at a time, then the eggs, one at a time. Then add the vanilla and milk. Beat on high speed just until well mixed.

3. BAKE THE CAKE. Pour the batter into the prepared pans and bake until a wooden pick comes out clean, 15 to 20 minutes for 8-inch pans, 12 to 15 minutes for 6-inch ones. Cool in the pans on a rack for 5 minutes, then flip the layers out onto the racks, removing the pans, and cool thoroughly.

continued

LEMON CURD FILLING

3 large lemons

1 cup sugar

5 large egg yolks

½ cup (1 stick) unsalted butter

LEMON CREAM CHEESE FROSTING

8 ounces soft cream cheese

½ cup (1 stick) soft, unsalted butter

⅛ teaspoon salt

Juice and grated zest of 1 lemon

¼ cup sifted confectioners' sugar, or to taste

4. **MAKE THE LEMON CURD.** While the cake is baking, in a medium heavy saucepan over medium heat, combine the grated lemon zest from 2 of the lemons with the sugar. Add the egg yolks and lemon juice to the sugar mixture and stir. Add the butter and stir until melted. Cook and stir until thick. Set aside to cool with a piece of wax paper set against the surface of the curd. Use to fill the cooled cake, spreading it generously between the layers.

5. **MAKE THE FROSTING.** While the cake is baking and cooling, combine the cream cheese, butter, salt, juice, zest, and sugar. Beat until stiff. Cover with a piece of wax paper, pressing it down against the top of the frosting. When the cake is cool, transfer one layer to a cake stand. Add one layer, top with the curd, and smooth it with an offset spatula. Add the second layer, secure it with toothpicks, and then frost the sides and top of the cooled cake. Store under a cake bell.

banana layer cake with walnut frosting

Moist, perfumed, and flecked with tiny banana seeds, this cake is a family favorite at our house. The aroma of banana when you cut into this sweet, tender cake will make your mouth water. The banana not only makes the cake taste great, it also gives it great keeping qualities.

baker's tip

> Choose brown, nearly over-the-top bananas for the cake batter, and firm but practically green bananas to slice between the layers. You'll get a more complex flavor and a fabulous texture from every bite this way.

3 large eggs

½ cup milk

½ cup vegetable oil

1 teaspoon fresh lemon juice

Grated zest of ½ lemon

2 cups mashed banana (about 3 medium)

3 cups sifted cake flour

1 cup granulated sugar

1 cup firmly packed dark brown sugar

1 teaspoon baking soda

½ teaspoon salt

1. **PREPARE TO BAKE.** Preheat the oven to 400°F. Spritz three or four 8-by-2-inch shiny round aluminum cake pans with Baker's Joy. Place the unbroken eggs in a bowl of hot tap water for 5 minutes before separating.

2. **MAKE THE BATTER.** Combine the milk, oil, lemon juice, zest, eggs, and mashed bananas in a large mixer bowl and mix well. Sift the flour, sugars, soda, and salt onto a sheet of wax paper. With the mixer running, spoon the flour into the wet ingredients. Mix just until blended.

3. **BAKE THE CAKE.** Divide the batter among the prepared pans, then bake for 15 minutes, or until a wooden pick comes out clean. Cool in the pan on a rack for 10 minutes, then flip the layers out onto a rack to cool.

continued

CREAM CHEESE FROSTING

8 ounces soft cream cheese

6 tablespoons soft, unsalted butter

3 cups sifted confectioners' sugar

½ teaspoon salt

Juice and zest of ½ lemon

1 teaspoon vanilla extract

2 firm, nearly green bananas, sliced thin

1½ cups chopped walnuts

4. MAKE THE FROSTING. Mix the cream cheese and butter in a bowl, and then stir in the confectioners' sugar and salt. Beat until fully incorporated. Stir in the lemon juice, zest, and vanilla.

5. FROST THE CAKE. Transfer one layer to a cake plate. Add a thin layer of frosting, top with a layer of thinly sliced bananas. Repeat until all the layers are iced. Ice the sides of the cake. Press the walnuts into the sides. Store the cake under a cake bell or covered in the refrigerator.

24 karat gold cake
with seven-minute icing

Of all the simple cakes I know, this is my favorite. Adding 10 egg yolks yields a rich, complex flavor. Choose organic eggs for the most intense golden color and taste. The texture is tender and buttery, and the hint of citrus adds a grace note that will, I believe, make this cake a favorite of yours, too, once you try it. Frost it with classic Seven-Minute Icing scented with more citrus, or top it with nothing more than a dusting of confectioners' sugar. If you want to make a luxe base for strawberry shortcake, this is it.

baker's tip

> When making this frosting, choose a double boiler or two heavy pans that fit one inside the other so that you can easily whisk the sugar and egg whites into a luscious white cloud. If you begin to feel the burn in your arm as you whisk away, just remember: You didn't have to pay a gym to get that strength training.

10 large egg yolks

2¼ cups sifted cake flour

½ teaspoon baking soda

½ teaspoon salt

1 teaspoon vanilla extract

1 teaspoon lemon or orange extract

1 cup buttermilk

1½ cups sugar, divided

¾ cup (1½ sticks) soft, unsalted butter

1. PREPARE TO BAKE. Arrange a rack in the middle of the oven and preheat it to 400°F. Place the egg yolks in a metal bowl and set it over a larger bowl of hot water. (You'll need 3 of the egg whites for the icing.) Spritz two 9-inch shiny round aluminum cake pans with Baker's Joy.

2. MAKE THE BATTER. Sift the flour, baking soda, and salt onto a piece of wax paper. Combine the vanilla and lemon extracts with the buttermilk in a glass measure. Beat the warmed egg yolks with an electric mixer on medium-high speed until thick and pale, about 5 minutes. Add ½ cup of the sugar, a tablespoon at a time, continuing to beat until the egg yolks form a ribbon, at least 3 minutes. Pinch off pieces of soft butter and toss into the egg yolks, continuing to beat. Add the remaining 1 cup sugar, a tablespoon at a time. Turn the mixer down to medium-low speed and add the flour and buttermilk mixtures alternately in thirds, starting with the flour and beating only until smooth.

continued

SEVEN-MINUTE ICING

3 large egg whites

¾ cup sugar

⅓ cup light corn syrup

Finely grated zest of 1 lemon or orange, plus extra for garnish

1 tablespoon fresh lemon or orange juice

¼ teaspoon cream of tartar

¼ teaspoon salt

3. BAKE THE CAKE. Divide the batter between the pans, smoothing the top with a spatula. Bake until golden brown and barely springing back at the touch, about 25 minutes, or until a toothpick inserted into the center comes out clean. Cool in the pans on a lightly greased rack for 5 minutes, then flip the layers out onto the rack and cool.

4. MAKE THE ICING. While the cake is cooling, make the icing. Fill the bottom of a double boiler one third full with water and bring to a boil over high heat. (Don't have a double boiler? Rig one using a pan and a stainless bowl or smaller pan that fits inside the larger pan on the bottom.) Add the egg whites, sugar, corn syrup, zest and juice, cream of tartar, and salt to the top pan. Set over the boiling water and whisk with a balloon whisk or a portable electric mixer until soft peaks form, about 7 minutes. Remove from the heat and continue to whisk for 2 minutes more, until the icing is thick and forms peaks whose tops droop over. Spread the warm icing between the layers and over the top of the cake-making swirls in the top. Coat the sides with the icing and finish with a grating of fresh lemon zest over the top. Store under a cake bell.

framboise-soaked génoise with lemon buttercream

This classic French cake seems dry by American standards, but the French have their reasons. Loving as they do to fuss with their food, they like to give this sturdy cake deep drinks of their favorite spirits. Here we have a luscious 6-inch cake, cooked quickly in a hot oven and desperate for a drink. Let the cake swill the liqueur of your choice. Stack the layers and finish with a tart lemon buttercream. I have stood local wild strawberries on their heads on top of this cake. On really special occasions, I some-times band the cake with a wide ribbon, which gets tossed once I start cutting the cake. This is the perfect little cake to take as a hostess gift—dramatic, precise, and much less work than the final result would suggest.

baker's tip

While the French pastry chef will whip the eggs and sugar over simmering water, we nanosecond Americans can achieve the same results by preheating the eggs in their shells in hot tap water and warming the sugar in the microwave for 10 seconds. Then break the eggs into the mixer's bowl and use the whisk attachment to whip the hell out of them. Once you've beaten the eggs and sugar into submission, the batter will fall away from the whisk in a passive, pliant, pale yellow ribbon. Crank the mixer up to high while you're mixing and it will work pretty fast, within 5 minutes. Then carefully sprinkle the flour mixture over the eggs and carefully fold it in, and finally paddle in the melted and cooled butter. Quickly transfer the batter to the baking pans, and voilà: In about 12 minutes, you'll have these adorable little layers. Wait 10 minutes so the heat can come out of them, and then let them drink deeply. While the cake layers cool, you can whip up the easy lemon buttercream. You'll wind up with a real tipsy cake. What could be better?

4 large eggs

2 tablespoons soft, unsalted butter

½ cup sugar, divided

1 cup sifted cake flour

⅛ teaspoon salt

1 teaspoon vanilla extract

1. **PREPARE TO BAKE.** Arrange the rack in the middle of the oven and preheat it to 400°F. Spritz two 6-inch shiny round aluminum cake pans with Baker's Joy. Place the unbroken eggs in a bowl of hot tap water. Melt the butter in a glass dish in the microwave for 20 seconds, and set aside. Place the sugar in a glass measure and heat in the microwave for 10 to 15 seconds.

2. **MAKE THE BATTER.** Sift the flour, 1 tablespoon of the sugar, and salt onto a piece of wax paper. Beat the eggs until light, then add the remaining sugar, a tablespoon at a time, beating continuously. Beat until the mixture has tripled in volume and is a lovely, airy pale yellow color, about 5 minutes. Test by lift-ing the whisk and observing the batter falling back in a ribbon that remains on

FRAMBOISE SYRUP

¼ cup water

¼ cup sugar

¼ cup framboise or other liqueur of your choice

LEMON BUTTERCREAM

⅓ cup (2 large) egg whites (see note)

⅔ cup sugar

¾ cup (1½ sticks) unsalted butter, cut into small pieces

1 tablespoon grated lemon zest

¼ cup fresh lemon juice

1 pint strawberries, stemmed

the surface for a moment. Add the vanilla during the last seconds of beating. Sprinkle half of the flour mixture over the eggs and barely fold it in with a rubber spatula. Repeat, folding in the remaining flour. Now drizzle the melted butter over the top and barely fold it in.

3. BAKE THE CAKE. Quickly transfer the batter to the prepared pan and bake until the cake begins to pull away from the sides, 12 to 18 minutes. Cool in the pan on a rack for 5 minutes, and then flip the layers out onto the rack to cool for 10 more minutes.

4. MAKE THE SYRUP. While the cake is cooling, combine the water and sugar in a small pan and bring to a boil, cooking until the sugar is dissolved. Off the heat, stir in the liqueur.

5. MAKE THE BUTTERCREAM. Place the unbroken eggs in a bowl of hot tap water for 5 minutes to warm them, then separate them and place the egg whites in a mixer bowl. (You won't need the yolks.) Add the sugar and whisk on high speed until stiff, glossy peaks form. Toss in the butter pieces and beat continuously. Add the lemon zest and juice and beat until smooth. Use immediately.

6. FINISH THE CAKE. Saw the cake in half horizontally, making two thin layers. Transfer the bottom layer of the cake to a cake plate. Pour half of the syrup over it, allowing it to soak in, and then frost with buttercream. Add the next layer. Pour the remaining syrup over it, let it soak in, and then frost with the remaining buttercream. Stand stemmed strawberries, point ups, shoulder to shoulder on the top. For special occasions, band the cake with a wide ribbon.

note: If you are concerned about raw egg whites, you may mix powdered egg whites (Just Whites or Wilton brands) and sugar in a bowl over simmering water until glossy peaks form. Cool slightly before adding the butter and finishing the recipe.

abraham lincoln's christmas gingerbread with orange-chocolate studded whipped cream

MAKES ONE 8-INCH SQUARE 2-LAYER CAKE, TO SERVE 10

Make this cake in a couple of 8-inch square pans for authenticity, but 9-inch round ones are fine if that's what you have. Floating between the layers and over the top is a cloud of chocolate and citrus–scented whipped cream. Abe was right. This is terrific for midwinter desserts. It's not too sweet and is redolent of spices.

baker's tip

Use fresh spices for best results. To keep track of your larder, mark the date you bought each spice, and throw it out after a year. For best quality, buy from Penzeys (see Mail-Order Sources, page 189). Their spices are as good as it gets and no more expensive than the grocery store's. To grate spices yourself, use a Microplane (see Mail-Order Sources, page 189), or a peppermill you have reserved for spices. And don't forget to use that Microplane on the citrus and chocolate too. It makes quick work of the frosting.

1 cup dark honey

1 teaspoon ground ginger

1 teaspoon ground cinnamon

½ teaspoon ground cloves

2½ cups sifted cake flour

1 teaspoon baking powder

½ teaspoon salt

½ cup (1 stick) soft, unsalted butter

1 teaspoon baking soda

½ cup firmly packed dark brown sugar

Grated zest of 1 lemon

1 large egg

1 cup buttermilk

1. PREPARE TO BAKE. Arrange the rack in the middle of the oven and preheat it to 400°F. Spritz two 8-inch square or 9-inch round shiny aluminum baking pans with Baker's Joy. Combine the honey, ginger, cinnamon, and cloves in a glass measure and bring to a boil in the microwave, about 1½ minutes. Set aside.

2. MAKE THE BATTER. Sift the flour, baking powder, and salt onto a piece of wax paper. Cream the butter, baking soda, and brown sugar in a stand mixer until light, about 3 minutes. Add the lemon zest and egg and mix again. Stir in the spiced honey. Add the flour mixture and buttermilk alternately in thirds, beating just until combined.

3. BAKE THE CAKE. Transfer the batter to the prepared pans and bake until a wooden pick comes out clean, about 20 minutes. Cool in the pans on a rack until the cakes begin to shrink from the sides, about 5 minutes, and then flip out onto the rack to cool completely.

continued

WHIPPED CREAM FROSTING

2 cups whipped cream

Grated rind of 1 orange

½ cup grated bittersweet chocolate

4. MAKE THE FROSTING. While the cake is baking, beat the cream to soft peaks, and then fold in the orange zest and chocolate. Cover and chill until ready to finish the cake. Arrange one layer of the cake on a plate and add a big jolt of whipped cream, smoothing it with an offset spatula. Add the last layer and frost the top and sides of the cake, smoothing the whipped cream with an offset spatula. Store in the refrigerator.

red velvet cake with royal icing

Legend has it that this cake was invented at the Waldorf-Astoria Hotel in New York in the teeth of the Depression. But it was quickly claimed by all cooks south of the Mason-Dixon Line and is known most fondly as a groom's cake in Methodist southern weddings, where the reception consists of a white bride's cake, some nonalcoholic punch, and a chocolate groom's cake. Remember the movie *Steel Magnolias*? The armadillo-shaped cake with the white icing and blood-red interior had to be a red velvet cake.

This mild cocoa cake is ramped up by a big jolt of red food coloring and finished with a thick coating of luscious, soft white icing.

baker's tip

Red food coloring stains, so take care to protect your clothes, and don't mix the cake using plastic utensils, unless you're eager to have red-tinted kitchen items. You'll get the best flavor by using Dutch process cocoa, but if you don't have it just use plain unsweetened cocoa. Note the old-fashioned, soft white frosting that finishes the cake. If you use a candy thermometer to measure the sugar syrup's cooking temperature, and a stand mixer to beat the egg whites, it's no big deal. If you own a Le Creuset saucepan with a lip (see Mail-Order Sources, page 189), now's the time to use it. It makes pouring that boiling syrup easy. Make the frosting while the cake bakes, then let it stand for 15 minutes while the cake cools before slathering it on the top and sides of the cake. Pure heaven.

2 large eggs

2¼ cups sifted cake flour

1 teaspoon salt

2 tablespoons unsweetened Dutch process cocoa powder

1 teaspoon baking powder

½ cup vegetable shortening

1½ cups sugar

1 cup buttermilk

2 tablespoons (1-ounce bottle) red food coloring

1 teaspoon vanilla extract

1 teaspoon white wine vinegar

1 teaspoon baking soda

1. **PREPARE TO BAKE.** Arrange the rack in the middle of the oven and preheat it to 400°F. Spritz two 9-inch shiny round aluminum cake pans with Baker's Joy. Place the unbroken eggs in a bowl of hot tap water.

2. **MAKE THE BATTER.** Sift the flour, salt, cocoa, and baking powder onto a piece of wax paper. Cream the shortening and sugar together in a mixer, beating for at least 4 minutes on high speed. Add the eggs, one at a time, and beat thoroughly after each addition.

Stir together the buttermilk, red food coloring, and vanilla in a glass measure. Add the buttermilk mixture to the flour mixture, alternately in thirds, beating on low speed. Turn off the mixer. Combine the vinegar and baking soda (it will foam), then fold it into the batter.

3. **BAKE THE CAKE.** Quickly pour the batter into the prepared pans and bake until a wooden pick comes out clean, about 15 minutes. Cool in the pans for 10 minutes on a rack, then flip out the layers onto the racks to cool completely.

continued

ROYAL ICING

1½ cups sugar

½ teaspoon cream of tartar

⅛ teaspoon salt

½ cup water

4 large egg whites

4. **MAKE THE ICING.** While the cake is baking, combine the sugar, cream of tartar, salt, and water in a small, heavy saucepan with a lip, such as Le Creuset. Cook over medium heat, stirring frequently, until the mixture is clear. Cook to 240°F (soft ball stage) on a candy thermometer. Meanwhile, beat the egg whites until soft peaks form, then slowly pour in the boiling sugar mixture and continue beating until the mixture forms stiff peaks. Turn off the mixer and let the icing stand while the cake cools.

5. **FINISH THE CAKE.** Transfer one layer to a cake plate and add a big dollop of icing. Spread with an offset spatula and then add the second layer. Secure to the bottom layer with 2 or 3 toothpicks. Ice the top and sides of the cake. Store under a cake bell.

triple chocolate orange passion cake

If you're looking for the *ne plus ultra* chocolate layer cake, try this one. Not only is it deep, dark, and mysterious, it also is aroused with the oil of the orange. If you wish to go the absolute extra mile, decorate the cake with orange or clementine segments dipped in melted bittersweet chocolate. It offers complete decadence without too much trouble, since it's made using a one-pot method that simply calls for you to add the ingredients, one after the other. How easy is that?

baker's tip

Citrus extract is available at grocery stores, but the orange oil from Boyajianinc (see Mail-Order Sources, page 189) will lift your baking efforts into the stratosphere. This fine company sells a variety of edible essential oils, which inform my cooking. The exquisite results will entrance any cook.

2 large eggs

2 ounces (2 squares) unsweetened chocolate

2 cups sifted cake flour

2 cups sugar

½ cup unsweetened Dutch process cocoa powder

1 teaspoon baking powder

½ teaspoon salt

½ cup milk

¼ cup vegetable oil

1 teaspoon vanilla extract

Grated zest and juice of 1 orange

1. PREPARE TO BAKE. Arrange the rack in the middle of the oven and preheat it to 400°F. Spritz two 9-inch or three 8-inch shiny aluminum round cake pans with Baker's Joy. Place the unbroken eggs in a bowl of hot tap water. Place the unsweetened chocolate squares in a glass dish and melt in the microwave on high power for about 1 minute.

2. MAKE THE BATTER. Sift the flour, sugar, cocoa, baking powder, and salt into a mixer bowl. Beat for 30 seconds, and then add—one at a time—the milk, oil, eggs, vanilla, and orange zest. Beat for 2 minutes at medium speed, scraping the sides of the bowl, then add enough boiling water to the orange juice to make 1 cup. Stir together with the melted chocolate and add to the batter. Stir just until blended.

3. BAKE THE CAKE. Divide the batter among the prepared pans and bake until a wooden pick comes out clean, 15 to 20 minutes. Cool in the pans on a rack for 5 minutes, then flip the layers out onto the rack to cool.

continued

CHOCOLATE ORANGE FROSTING

6 tablespoons soft, unsalted butter

1 pound (1 box) sifted confectioners' sugar, divided

½ cup whipping cream

¼ teaspoon salt

¼ teaspoon orange oil or extract

2 ounces bittersweet chocolate

Clementine or orange slices, for decoration (optional)

Bittersweet chocolate, for dipping (optional)

4. MAKE THE FROSTING. While the cake is baking, cream the butter with half of the confectioners' sugar, then add the cream, remaining confectioners' sugar, salt, and orange oil. Melt the chocolate in the microwave on high power (about 1 minute), then scoop it into the frosting and continue beating until smooth and fluffy. Let the frosting stand while the cake cools.

5. FINISH THE CAKE. Transfer the bottom layer of the cake to a cake plate and add a big dollop of frosting and smooth with an offset spatula. Secure the layer(s) with toothpicks, then frost the top and sides with the remaining frosting. Garnish with clementine or orange slices around the base of the cake if you wish. If you'd like, to dip the fruits, simply melt a couple of ounces of bittersweet chocolate in the microwave and dip away. This won't take more than a couple of minutes, and the results are outstanding.

2

Tube and Bundt
CAKES

Tube cakes. Bundt cakes. Why do we like them? They present well. A dusting of confectioner's sugar, or a smattering of spirits, or perhaps a simple glaze is often all the finish they need. They speak for themselves. Often ravishing with fruits and nuts, they'll serve 16, so they're great to take to a party. And, using this new technique, it doesn't take an hour or more to bake them.

The Bundt cake originated in Europe—exactly where is lost in the flour dust of baking history, but it was probably in Germany or Austria, where it was known as the kugelhopf. The traditional pan had a tube or "chimney" in the middle to make the heavy, dense yeast batter cook more quickly and evenly. It took an enterprising Minneapolis entrepreneur, a homesick immigrant, and an American housewife to create the category we call Bundt cake, which is a cake quickly lightened with eggs and baking powder instead of the tedious, time-consuming yeast used by European bakers.

In 1950, the Minnesota owners, Dave and Dotty Dalquist, of the newly minted Nordic Ware Corporation, who had started the business in 1946 in their basement with $500 and a dream, were presented with a challenge. One of their friends, the president of the local Hadassah chapter, a Jewish women's organization, asked them to try to re-create the traditional fluted tube pan she remembered from her German-Jewish grandmother's kitchen in the Old Country before the dislocations of World War II.

Originally called a "Bund" pan (*bund* means "gathering," and the fancy fluted shape of the pan seemed best suited to cakes baked for celebrations), the pan got a needed boost in sales in 1966, when a Houston housewife, Ella Rita Helfrich, invented a cake recipe using the pan and won the Pillsbury Bake-off. Mrs. Helfrich's recipe took the country by cake, put the Bundt cake pan on the map, and changed forever the landscape of boutique baker's cases in America. (See page 56 for Mrs. Helfrich's Tunnel of Fudge cake recipe.)

Now the Bundt cake pan is called "the most popular baking mold in the world," and it is estimated that more than 45 million are tucked away in American kitchens today.

Want to explore the possibilities? See the expanded choices available from Nordic Ware today (see Mail-Order Sources, page 189). They keep coming up with cool, new shapes with ruffles and flourishes fit for the fanciest fairy tale cake, and the pans are still the gold standard for cast aluminum Bundt pans. Stick with their brand and you won't be disappointed. Like other heavy-gauge aluminum baking pans, they heat up quickly and cool down quickly. You'll get a cake that has a lovely, even crumb and a glorious golden crust.

Smooth-sided tube pans, on the other hand, designed to conduct heat to the center of the batter, are not only excellent for heavy-battered pound cakes or fruit and nut cakes, but also are the answer to perfect angel food and chiffon cakes that rely on steam and air to lift them. These fragile batters work only when placed in squeaky-clean shiny aluminum tube pans with removable bottoms. The chimney gives an additional surface for those cakes to climb in their rush to glory. Although you can buy aluminum tube pans without removable bottoms, those are best suited to heavy batters that call for a spritzing of Baker's Joy. For angels and chiffons, choose a pan with a removable bottom. If your pan doesn't have three legs to stand on while it cools, simply prop its tube on a wine or soda pop bottle so it can cool quickly.

When you think about the way batters work, think about bubble gum. You chew it, you warm it up, you introduce liquid, then you blow air into it and it forms a fine yet sturdy bubble. Cake batter works the same way. You mix the ingredients, then the cake rises based upon the air you beat into it, the eggs in the batter, and perhaps the addition of baking powder or soda, which creates a chemical reaction when placed in the hot oven (think tiny bombs going off). That yields CO_2, which gets trapped into each cell of the cake and then hardened off as the cake cooks and dries out.

And remember, the more delicate the cake batter, the more help it needs. Use the proper technique, the proper aluminum pan, and the proper oven temperature, and you will be rewarded with a satisfying cake. And hey, even if it isn't perfect, it will still taste good. You can always make another one next week to work on your technique.

The tube, or chimney in the middle of the pan, aids in getting heat right to the heart of your cake so that it can blow up like a great balloon and lift off light as a cloud.

Bon voyage.

praline pound fudge cake

The original pound cakes had a pound of each ingredient, but now that we measure by volume, we don't even know how much a pound is. This particular southern version is luxurious with brown sugar and pecans that become a crisp praline crust simply by being sprinkled on the bottom of the cake pan. Who knew praline could be so simple? The texture is somewhere between fudge and a great New York cheesecake. Nestle each slice in a pool of warm caramel sauce, homemade or store-bought, for the ultimate indulgence.

baker's tip

For the best flavor development and ease in slicing, always make pound cake at least 8 hours before you're ready to serve. Store it in a tin or other airtight container and the cake will remain fresh for a week or more.

1½ cups chopped pecans, divided

6 large eggs

1½ cups (3 sticks) soft, unsalted butter

8 ounces soft cream cheese

2 cups firmly packed dark brown sugar

3 cups sifted cake flour

½ teaspoon salt

2 teaspoons vanilla extract

CARAMEL SAUCE (OPTIONAL)

1 cup sugar

3 tablespoons heavy cream

3 tablespoons unsalted butter

1. **PREPARE TO BAKE.** Arrange the rack in the middle of the oven and preheat it to 400°F. Spritz a 10-inch tube pan with Baker's Joy. Sprinkle ½ cup of the chopped pecans over the bottom and sides of the pan. Place the unbroken eggs in a bowl of hot tap water.

2. **MAKE THE BATTER.** Cream the butter and cream cheese in a mixer until light, then add the brown sugar and continue beating for 5 minutes. Add the eggs, one at a time, mixing well after each. Spoon in the flour and salt, and mix just until blended. Don't overmix. Fold in the vanilla and the remaining cup of pecans.

3. **BAKE THE CAKE.** Spoon the batter into the prepared pan and bake until a wooden pick comes out clean, about 35 minutes. Cool the cake in the pan on a rack for 10 minutes, then remove it from the pan to cool on the rack completely.

4. **MAKE THE CARAMEL SAUCE.** In a dry, heavy 5-quart saucepan, cook the sugar over medium-low heat until the sugar begins to melt and turn golden. Tip the pan to melt all of the sugar. Remove from the heat and add the cream and butter. Stir vigorously. Simmer just until the mixture is dissolved. Store in a jar, covered, in the refrigerator.

5. **SERVE THE CAKE.** Drizzle a tablespoon of caramel sauce onto each dessert plate if you wish, then add a slice of cake.

tunnel of fudge cake

Back to the future with the cake that won the Pillsbury Bake-Off in 1966, when a woman from Houston named Ella Rita Helfrich discovered that by adding a package of powdered frosting to a cake, she got a tunnel of fudge. The magic of the cake, then and now, is that the edges are crisp and crunchy and the center is, indeed, fudge. Now this is pure food science and the secret is in the ingredients. The cake Ella Rita made used a powdered icing product that Pillsbury soon took off the market. Tunnel of Fudge lovers screamed. So the Pillsbury test kitchen deconstructed the mix and found that it was nothing but confectioners' sugar and cocoa. They figured that by adding those ingredients to the cake they could give the old winner a new life. Guess what? The new version is even better. Nothing more is required but a dusting of confectioners' sugar to finish it.

baker's tip

Make the cake in an aluminum Bundt pan, crank that oven up to 400°F, and you'll not only knock 30 percent off the cooking time, but you'll also improve the crumb and the finished product. Don't worry about finding an aluminum Bundt pan. You can see numerous choices within the category at the Nordic Ware factory (see Mail-Order Sources, page 189). Whether you want a traditional fluted cake, a cathedral shape, or even a flower, the choices keep on multiplying at the Nordic Ware factory. You can also make mini-Bundts. Follow the baking directions that come with the pans for the smaller cakes and present each guest with his or her own individual cake.

6 large eggs

1¾ cups (3½ sticks) soft, unsalted butter

1¾ cups granulated sugar

2 cups confectioners' sugar, plus more for dusting

2¼ cups sifted cake flour

¾ cup unsweetened Dutch process cocoa powder

2 cups chopped walnuts

1. PREPARE TO BAKE. Arrange the rack in the middle of the oven and preheat it to 400°F. Spritz a 12-cup Bundt pan with Baker's Joy. Place the unbroken eggs in a bowl of hot tap water.

2. MAKE THE BATTER. Cream the butter with the granulated sugar in a mixer until fluffy and light, about 3 minutes. Break the eggs in, one at a time, beating well after each addition. Sprinkle in the confectioners' sugar, beating still. Sift the flour and cocoa onto a piece of wax paper, and then scoop into the batter. Blend well, then fold in the nuts.

3. BAKE THE CAKE. Spoon the batter into the prepared Bundt pan and bake on the middle rack of the hot oven for 35 minutes. (No wooden pick inserted into this cake will ever come out clean. There is that underground river of fudge in the middle, forever liquid treasure.)

4. FINISH THE CAKE. Cool the cake in the pan on a rack for 10 minutes, and then flip it over onto the rack. Lift off the pan and cool completely. Sprinkle with confectioners' sugar and serve.

florida sunshine cake

This citrusy chiffon cake freckled with orange zest melts in your mouth and can be made using orange, tangerine, honeybell, tangelo, lemon, or lime juice and zest. Each particular fruit gives its own particular zip. For a cake as light as a gulf breeze, you need to understand that the success of this kind of cake relies on captured air and steam. Properly done, this cake is a first cousin to the angel food cake. It isn't hard to make; it just follows a different process from the usual butter cake. Fold the yolk mixture into the whites with the lightest hand. You'll note that it looks a lot like the angel food cakes they sell in the supermarket, but wait until you taste it. You'll see why they call Florida the sunshine state.

baker's tip

The best pan to use here is a 10-inch shiny aluminum angel food cake pan with a removable bottom. Make sure the pan is squeaky clean before adding the batter, because the cake climbs up the sides of the pan in its last thrust skyward and hangs on for dear life, unless you've made the pan greasy with unwanted fat. Once the cake is baked, turn it upside down in the pan over a rack and let it cool completely before removing it from the pan. Run a thin-bladed knife around the edges and down the sides of the tube. The pan should easily lift away from the cake.

6 large eggs

1½ cups sifted cake flour

1¼ cups sugar, divided

1 tablespoon baking powder

1 teaspoon salt

Grated zest of ½ orange or other citrus of your choice

½ cup vegetable oil

¼ cup orange juice

½ cup water

½ teaspoon cream of tartar

GLAZE

8 ounces (½ box) sifted confectioners' sugar

2 tablespoons orange juice

Grated zest of ½ orange

1 tablespoon lemon juice

Grated zest of ½ lemon

½ teaspoon salt

1. **PREPARE TO BAKE.** Arrange the rack in the middle of the oven and heat it to 400°F. Place the unbroken eggs in a bowl of hot tap water.

2. **MAKE THE BATTER.** Sift together the flour, 1 cup of the sugar, baking powder, and salt into a large bowl. Sprinkle the zest over it and toss to mix. Separate the eggs. Make a well in the center of the flour and add—in order—the oil, egg yolks, orange juice, and water. Whisk with a wire whisk until smooth. In a large mixer bowl, beat the egg whites until foamy, then add the cream of tartar and beat until stiff, adding the remaining ¼ cup sugar, a spoonful at a time. Fold the batter into the egg whites, taking care not to overmix. Pour into an ungreased 10-inch shiny aluminum tube pan, preferably with a removable bottom.

3. **BAKE THE CAKE.** Bake until golden, 30 to 35 minutes. Invert the cake over a rack and cool completely. Run a thin blade around the edges and the tube, and then carefully lift off the pan.

4. **FINISH THE CAKE.** In a medium bowl, whisk together the glaze ingredients and then drizzle over the cake. Store under a cake bell.

edith's pound cake

MAKES ONE 10-INCH BUNDT OR TUBE CAKE, TO SERVE 16

When a recipe gets as popular as Edith Sakell's mother's pound cake, and the requests for it come fast and furious, it's natural that a few corners get cut. When she needs to make one, Edith claims to pitch in the ingredients with wild abandon. She can have this cake in the oven in 7 minutes. And once it's out, there's no need for frosting. Edith just dusts it with confectioners' sugar and serves it along with ice cream and fresh fruit of the season. This recipe is pure old-fashioned southern: moist, sweet, and redolent of vanilla and almond. Change to lemon flavoring if you wish by substituting the grated zest and juice of 1 lemon for the extracts.

baker's tip

The only caveat Edith has is this: Don't overbake it. It's better a little underdone. You've probably seen similar recipes, sometimes called "cold oven" pound cake. But I've found that preheating the oven to 400°F not only speeds up the cooking, but also makes for a luscious golden crust. That cold oven may have come about because old-fashioned bakers got the batter made before the wood stove had heated up, and they just threw it in—what the heck. So if you forget to preheat, don't worry. Just add time to the cooking period.

6 large eggs

1 cup (2 sticks) soft, unsalted butter

3 cups sugar

1 tablespoon vanilla extract

1 tablespoon almond extract, or the juice and grated zest of 1 lemon

3 cups sifted cake flour

1 cup whipping cream

Confectioners' sugar, for dusting

Whipped cream and fresh fruit, for serving

1. PREPARE TO BAKE. Arrange the rack in the middle of the oven and preheat it to 400°F. Spritz a 10-inch tube or 12-cup Bundt pan with Baker's Joy. Place the unbroken eggs in a bowl of hot tap water.

2. MAKE THE BATTER. Place the butter in the bowl of a mixer and start to cream it, adding the sugar, then the vanilla and almond extracts, and then the eggs—one at a time, followed by the flour. Pour in the cream. Once it's thoroughly mixed, it's ready.

3. BAKE THE CAKE. Transfer the batter to the prepared pan and bake until a wooden pick comes out clean, about 35 minutes. Cool in the pan on a rack for 5 minutes, and then flip it out onto the rack to cool completely.

4. FINISH THE CAKE. Dust with confectioners' sugar and serve alongside whipped cream and fresh fruit of the season.

lemon buttermilk cake with a citrus glaze

Tender as young love, with just enough citrus zip to keep it interesting, this puckery cake needs no embellishment, but if you insist, nestle a few fresh, glorious strawberries around the edges.

baker's tip

Because this cake has buttermilk and lemon juice, it needs both baking soda and baking powder to lift it to its heights. Be sure to use products you have purchased within the last six months, for best results. And remember, double-acting means that the first part of the baking powder's chemical reaction takes place when you add liquid to the flour, and the second takes place when the cake batter encounters that blast of heat from a properly preheated oven. Place the cake in the oven promptly to get the maximum effect.

4 large eggs
1 cup (2 sticks) soft, unsalted butter
2 cups sugar
1 cup buttermilk
2 tablespoons lemon juice
Grated zest of ½ lemon
3 cups sifted cake flour
½ teaspoon baking soda
½ teaspoon baking powder
½ teaspoon salt

CITRUS GLAZE
8 ounces (½ box) confectioners' sugar
5 tablespoons lemon juice
Grated zest of ½ lemon
5 tablespoons orange juice
Grated zest of ½ orange
¼ teaspoon salt

1. **PREPARE TO BAKE.** Arrange the rack in the middle of the oven and preheat it to 400°F. Spritz a 10-inch tube pan with Baker's Joy and set aside. Place the unbroken eggs in a bowl of hot tap water.

2. **MAKE THE BATTER.** Cream the butter and sugar in a mixer until light, and then break in the eggs, one at a time, mixing well after each addition. In a glass measure, stir together the buttermilk, lemon juice, and zest. Sift the flour together with the baking soda, baking powder, and salt onto a piece of wax paper, then add to the butter mixture, a spoonful at a time, alternately with the buttermilk.

3. **BAKE THE CAKE.** Pour the batter into the prepared pan and bake until a wooden pick comes out clean, 30 to 35 minutes. Cool in the pan on a rack for 10 minutes, then flip it out onto the rack to cool completely.

4. **FINISH THE CAKE.** Whisk together the confectioners' sugar, citrus juices, zest, and salt. Drizzle over the top and sides of the cake.

lemon sweet potato bundt cake with a browned butter glaze

Sweet potatoes make an interesting addition to cake. Not only does the cake taste good, but it keeps well. Start with a fresh sweet potato and cook it in the microwave until tender, then peel and mash or, even simpler, just buy two 15-ounce cans of sweet potato, drain, and mash. The cake will have a lovely caramel color and a complex flavor from the marriage of citrus and spices.

baker's tip

Find only yams at the store? Go ahead and buy them. They're probably sweet potatoes, since yams are rarely sold in North America. In fact, however, either root vegetable will work. Both yams and sweet potatoes are the roots of tropical plants, the sweet potato being a cousin to the morning glory, *Ipomoea batatas* to be exact, while the yam is an African derivative of the genus *Dioscorea*.

3 large eggs

½ cup milk

½ cup vegetable oil

1 teaspoon fresh lemon juice

Grated zest of ½ lemon

2 cups cooked, mashed sweet potatoes

3 cups sifted cake flour

1 cup granulated sugar

1 cup firmly packed dark brown sugar

1 teaspoon baking soda

½ teaspoon salt

1 teaspoon ground ginger

1 teaspoon ground cinnamon

½ teaspoon ground cloves

BROWNED BUTTER GLAZE

¼ cup (½ stick) unsalted butter

2 cups sifted confectioners' sugar

½ teaspoon salt

2 tablespoons milk

1 teaspoon lemon juice

Grated zest of ½ lemon

1. **PREPARE TO BAKE.** Arrange the rack in the middle of the oven and preheat it to 400°F. Spritz a 10-inch Bundt or tube pan with Baker's Joy and set aside. Place the unbroken eggs in a bowl of hot tap water.

2. **MAKE THE BATTER.** Combine the milk, oil, lemon juice, zest, eggs, and mashed sweet potatoes in a stand mixer. Mix well. Sift the flour, sugars, baking soda, salt, and spices onto a sheet of wax paper and then, with the mixer running, spoon into the wet ingredients. Mix just until well combined.

3. **BAKE THE CAKE.** Transfer the batter to the prepared pan, and bake until a wooden pick comes out clean, 30 to 35 minutes. Cool in the pan on a rack for 10 minutes, then flip it over onto a rack to cool.

4. **MAKE THE GLAZE.** Place the butter in a small saucepan and heat until it browns. Meanwhile, place the confectioners' sugar and salt in a medium bowl. Whisk in the butter, then add just enough milk, lemon juice, and zest to make a thin glaze. Drizzle over the warm cake. Serve warm or cold.

two-toned pecan bundt cake
with a bourbon molasses glaze

First cousin to a marble cake, this two-toned, two-flavored cake is delicious to start with. But soak this cake with a perfumed whiskey glaze, and it will keep exceptionally well. Make it up to 3 days before serving, and don't forget to pick up a pint of best-quality ice cream to accompany it.

baker's tip To get the most flavor from nuts, pan-roast them. It's easy. Place the nuts in a small, dry skillet. Heat over medium-high heat until the nuts begin to color and give off their distinctive aroma. Immediately transfer them to a bowl so they don't make that fatal leap from toasted to burned.

4 large eggs
1 cup chopped pecans
1 cup (2 sticks) soft, unsalted butter
2 cups sugar
2 teaspoons vanilla extract
3¼ cups sifted cake flour
2 teaspoons baking powder
¾ teaspoon salt
1 cup whole milk
¼ cup light corn syrup
¼ cup full-flavored molasses
½ teaspoon baking soda

1. **PREPARE TO BAKE.** Arrange the rack in the center of the oven and preheat it to 400°F. Spritz a 10-inch Bundt cake pan with Baker's Joy. Place the unbroken eggs in a bowl of hot tap water. Pan-roast the pecans (see Baker's Tip, above).

2. **MAKE THE BATTER.** Cream the butter in a stand mixer on high speed until light, about 2 minutes. Add the sugar and continue beating. Add the vanilla. Beat in the eggs, one at a time, and continue mixing until fluffy, about 3 minutes.

Sift the flour, baking powder, and salt onto a piece of wax paper. Add to the butter mixture in thirds, alternately with the milk. Transfer half of the batter (it will be heavy) to the prepared pan.

Stir together the pecans, corn syrup, molasses, and baking soda, and then fold into the remaining cake batter. Spoon on top of the first cake batter in the pan.

3. **BAKE THE CAKE.** Bake until a wooden pick inserted in the center of the cake comes out clean, 35 to 40 minutes. Cool in the pan on a rack for 10 minutes, then flip it out onto the rack to cool completely.

BOURBON MOLASSES GLAZE

1 teaspoon water

½ teaspoon baking soda

1 cup sugar

½ cup buttermilk

½ cup (1 stick) unsalted butter

1 teaspoon full-flavored molasses

½ cup bourbon

1 teaspoon vanilla extract

Butter pecan ice cream,
for serving (optional)

4. MAKE THE GLAZE. Stir the water and baking soda together in a small bowl. Bring the sugar, buttermilk, butter, and molasses to a boil in a heavy saucepan over high heat, stirring to dissolve the sugar and melt the butter. Reduce the heat to medium and stir in the baking soda mixture (it will bubble). Boil until golden and a little thicker, about 5 minutes. Remove from the heat and stir in the bourbon and vanilla.

5. FINISH THE CAKE. Transfer the cake to a cake plate and drizzle half of the hot glaze over the cake, allowing it to soak in. Pour the remaining glaze into a pitcher, cover, and refrigerate. Store in a cake bell. Just before serving, heat the sauce in the microwave for about 20 seconds, pool it onto dessert plates, add a slice of cake, and serve with ice cream if you wish.

rummy prune spice cake
with bacardi butter rum glaze

MAKES ONE 10-INCH BUNDT
CAKE, TO SERVE 16

Spicy, not too sweet, and rich with both prunes and nuts, this cake keeps well and makes a fine finish to a cold-weather dinner.

baker's tip } Use the freshest spices to get the best flavor from this or other baked goods. Order from Penzeys (see Mail-Order Sources, page 189) and you'll have the very best.

4 large eggs

2 cups pitted, quartered prunes

2 tablespoons Bacardi Gold rum

1 cup (2 sticks) soft, unsalted butter

1½ cups sugar

3 cups sifted cake flour

1 teaspoon ground cinnamon

1 teaspoon ground cloves

1 teaspoon ground nutmeg

2 teaspoons baking soda

¼ teaspoon salt

½ cup milk

1 cup chopped walnuts

BACARDI BUTTER RUM GLAZE

¼ cup (½ stick) soft, unsalted butter

¾ cup sugar

3 tablespoons Bacardi Gold rum

3 tablespoons water

¼ teaspoon salt

½ cup finely chopped walnuts

1 teaspoon vanilla extract

1. **PREPARE TO BAKE.** Arrange the rack in the middle of the oven and preheat it to 400°F. Spritz a 12-cup Bundt pan with Baker's Joy. Place the unbroken eggs in a bowl of hot tap water. Cover the prunes with water and rum and boil until soft, about 10 minutes. Drain.

2. **MAKE THE BATTER.** Cream the butter and sugar together in a stand mixer until light. Add the eggs, one at a time, and beat until the mixture is very light. Sift the flour with the cinnamon, cloves, nutmeg, baking soda, and salt onto a piece of wax paper. Add the flour mixture to the butter mixture in thirds, alternately with the milk. Don't overbeat. Stop when all the ingredients are incorporated. Fold in the drained prunes and walnuts, using a rubber spatula.

3. **BAKE THE CAKE.** Pour the batter into the prepared pan and bake until a wooden pick comes out clean and the cake begins to shrink from the sides of the pan, 30 to 35 minutes. Let it cool in the pan on a rack for 10 minutes, and then flip it onto the rack to cool completely.

4. **GLAZE THE CAKE.** Combine the butter, sugar, rum, water, salt, and walnuts in a small saucepan over high heat and bring to a boil, then boil for 3 minutes. Remove from the heat. Stir in the vanilla. Pour over the cake, top and sides as well as the middle, while the glaze is warm. Store at room temperature under a cake bell.

jack daniel's fruit and nut cake

Want to give gifts from your kitchen this holiday? Nothing would be more welcome than this old-fashioned whiskey cake. It's basically what fruitcake ought to be but usually isn't: sweet, tart, rich, and redolent of spirits. Not only is this cake great with tea, you can slice and toast it for breakfast—on, say, Christmas morning—and it's a winner as well on the sideboard because it keeps for weeks. If you wish to substitute other dried fruits, do so measure for measure. Try apricots, prunes, peaches, or apples.

baker's tip

To prevent toughening of the cake, don't overmix it. Set the mixer on medium-high speed to cream the butter, sugar, and eggs, and then turn it to low to incorporate the flour and whiskey. Stop the instant the flour is mixed in for a meltingly tender crumb.

6 large eggs

1 cup (2 sticks) soft, unsalted butter

2 cups sugar

4 cups sifted cake flour, divided

1 tablespoon baking powder

2 teaspoons ground nutmeg

1 teaspoon salt

1 cup Jack Daniel's or other good aged whiskey

15 ounces (1 box) golden raisins

1 cup currants

4 cups pecan pieces

1. PREPARE TO BAKE. Arrange the rack in the middle of the oven and preheat it to 400°F. Spritz a 12-cup Bundt or loaf pan (or smaller pans; see step 3) with Baker's Joy. Place the unbroken eggs in a bowl of hot tap water.

2. MAKE THE BATTER. Cream the butter and sugar in a stand mixer until fluffy, and then break the eggs, one at a time, into the mixture. Beat until well combined. Sift 3½ cups of the flour, the baking powder, nutmeg, and salt onto a piece of wax paper, then add to the butter mixture in thirds, alternately with the whiskey, mixing on low speed just until the mixture is combined. Place the raisins, currants, nuts, and remaining ½ cup flour in a plastic bag. Shake to mix thoroughly, and then fold into the batter by hand.

3. BAKE THE CAKE. Transfer the batter to the prepared pan(s). Fill smaller pans three fourths full. Place the cake(s) on the middle rack of the hot oven and cook until a wooden pick comes out clean and the top springs back at the touch:

For a large Bundt or loaf cake: 35 to 40 minutes

For 2 smaller loaves: 20 to 25 minutes

For 8 mini-Bundts: 15 to 20 minutes

Cool in the pans on a rack for 5 minutes, then flip out onto the rack to cool.

continued

WHISKEY GLAZE

¼ cup (½ stick) soft, unsalted butter

2 cups sifted confectioners' sugar

½ teaspoon salt

3 tablespoons Jack Daniel's or other good aged whiskey

4. MAKE THE GLAZE. Heat the butter in a small skillet until it browns. Combine the confectioners' sugar and salt in a medium bowl, and then add the butter and whiskey. Stir to mix, and then drizzle over the cake(s). Store in airtight tin(s).

old-fashioned fresh apple cake

New York State's Red Rome apples will yield a sweet-tart cake that has a splendid flavor. Other good choices include Macoun, Braeburn, McIntosh, or Gala apples. The worst choices include (not so) Delicious apples from Washington. The main idea is to choose a tart-sweet apple with firm flesh. For the most complex flavor and texture, combine two or three apple varieties.

baker's tip

> For best results, don't peel the apples; just coarsely grate them whole, using a box grater or the food processor. The cake will have better texture and nice red flecks in it.

4 apples, cored

Juice and grated zest of 1 lemon

3 large eggs

3 cups sifted cake flour

1 tablespoon baking powder

1 teaspoon baking soda

1 teaspoon salt

1 tablespoon freshly ground cinnamon

2 cups sugar

1 cup vegetable oil

2 teaspoons vanilla extract

1 cup walnuts or pecans

Confectioners' sugar, for dusting

1. **PREPARE TO BAKE.** Arrange the rack in the middle of the oven and then preheat it to 400°F. Spritz a 10-inch tube or Bundt pan with Baker's Joy and set aside. Grate the apples, then spritz them with the lemon juice and zest and set aside. Place the unbroken eggs in a bowl of hot tap water.

2. **MAKE THE BATTER.** Sift the flour, baking powder, baking soda, salt, and cinnamon onto a piece of wax paper. Break the eggs into the mixer, set it on high speed, then add the sugar, beating well. Pour in the oil and vanilla. Spoon in the flour mixture and mix until well blended. (It will be heavy.) Fold the grated apples into the cake batter, along with the nuts.

3. **BAKE THE CAKE.** Pour the batter into the prepared pan. Bake until a wooden pick comes out clean, 30 to 35 minutes. Cool in the pan on a rack for 10 minutes, then turn the cake out onto a cake stand. Dust with confectioners' sugar. Store under a cake bell.

3

Single-Layer
CAKES

The cakes in this chapter are rich, dense, and sumptuous, the kind that take only a sliver to satisfy. Some are made with nuts in place of the flour or, in one case, with cocoa for flour. Almost as rich as candy while not being overly sweet, these cakes make a big splash. Use a springform pan, or an ordinary cake pan if that's all you have. Carefully prepare the pan with a big spritz of Baker's Joy to release the just-baked cake from the pan.

You'll note a preponderance of chocolate cakes here. There's a reason for this. Who doesn't love a deep, intense chocolate experience? The single-layer cake, carefully made and perfumed and flavored in a variety of ways, makes the almost perfect dessert.

Use the best chocolate you can find. You will be richly rewarded.

butter almond cake
with lemon curd

This rich, buttery single-layer cake is pungent with the crunch of toasted, salted ground almonds and is both sweet and tart with the addition of lemon curd. Simply spoon the lemon curd onto the batter, top with more almonds, and bake.

baker's tip

Basically, this cake has the frosting baked with it. Start off by making the world's easiest lemon curd. No double boiler, no tedious process, just whisk away and pull it off the heat the instant it thickens. Transfer to a flat plate and refrigerate. You'll have some left over. Good—spread it on tomorrow's toast.

LEMON CURD

Grated zest and juice of 2 large lemons

¾ cup sugar

¼ teaspoon salt

4 large eggs

6 tablespoons (¾ stick) unsalted butter, cut into chunks

1. MAKE THE LEMON CURD. In a medium, heavy saucepan, stir together the lemon zest, juice, and sugar until the sugar dissolves. Stir in the salt and eggs and whisk until smooth. Add the butter. Over medium heat, and whisking *constantly*, cook until the mixture thickens and just begins to boil, about 3 minutes. Pour instantly into a 9-inch glass pie plate. Cover with plastic wrap, pressing the wrap onto the curd but leaving the edges loose (so the steam can escape). Place in the refrigerator.

2. PREPARE TO BAKE. Arrange the rack in the middle of the oven and heat it to 400°F. Spritz a 9-inch springform pan with Baker's Joy. Pulse the almonds in a food processor until dry and powdery, and then divide into 2 parts, ½ cup and ¼ cup. Warm the unbroken eggs in a bowl of hot tap water.

BUTTER ALMOND CAKE

¾ cup roasted, salted almonds (divided)

2 large eggs

½ cup (1 stick) soft, unsalted butter

1 cup sugar

1 cup sifted cake flour

1 teaspoon baking powder

½ teaspoon salt

2 tablespoons water

Whipped cream, for serving

3. **MAKE THE BATTER.** Cream the butter and sugar in a stand mixer until light and fluffy. Sift the flour, baking powder, and salt onto a piece of wax paper. Sprinkle over the top of the butter mixture. Run the mixer on low until mixed. Whisk the eggs and water together in a small bowl and add to the butter mixture. Turn the mixer to high speed and mix until thoroughly blended. Fold in ½ cup of the ground almonds and mix again just until blended.

4. **BAKE THE CAKE.** Turn the cake batter into the prepared pan. Drop about 8 tablespoons of the lemon curd around the edges and 3 to 4 tablespoons in the middle. Smooth the top to completely cover the cake batter. Sprinkle with the remaining ¼ cup ground almonds. Bake until a wooden pick comes out clean (be sure to dig past the curd, which will be runny until it cools), 15 to 20 minutes. Cool in the pan on a rack for 10 minutes, then run a thin-bladed knife around the perimeter, remove the sides of the pan, and cool completely.

5. **TO SERVE,** cut the cake into wedges and serve with a jot of whipped cream.

new york cheesecake

This is the real deal. Honest to the Big Apple New York Cheesecake starts baking at an even higher temperature than we've been using. After the crust bakes at 325°F, the cheesecake is started at 500°F to give that dense cream cheese and egg mixture a chance to really get a blast of heat. Then it is turned down to 225°F for a long, slow finish. It's worth the wait. This is dense, tangy, and sweet. A regular brick of a cheesecake for those who grew up on Junior's famous cheesecakes in Brooklyn.

baker's tip

Eat this cheesecake plain or fancy. Top it with blueberry or cherry preserves, if you wish. Use Nabisco Chocolate Wafers for the crust instead of graham crackers. But whatever you do, remember to dip the blade of the serrated cutting knife in hot water so it will cut into neat slices.

GRAHAM CRACKER OR CHOCOLATE WAFER CRUST

1 cup crumbs (8 graham crackers or chocolate wafers whizzed in the food processor)

1 tablespoon sugar

6 tablespoons (¾ stick), plus more for pan, unsalted butter, melted

1. PREPARE TO BAKE. Arrange the rack in the middle of the oven and preheat it to 325°F. Toss the crumbs with the sugar. Add the melted butter and toss to mix. Brush the bottom and sides of a 9-inch springform pan with additional melted butter, then pour in the crumbs and press evenly over the bottom, using your knuckles to press the mixture down tight. Bake until the aroma makes you weak in the knees and the crust is beginning to brown, about 12 minutes. Cool on a rack.

continued

CHEESECAKE FILLING

2½ pounds soft cream cheese

⅛ teaspoon salt

1½ cups sugar

½ cup sour cream

2 teaspoons lemon juice

Grated zest of ½ lemon

2 teaspoons vanilla extract

8 large eggs, divided

Fruit preserves, for serving (optional)

2. MAKE THE CHEESECAKE FILLING. Turn the oven temperature up to 500°F. Beat the cream cheese at medium speed in a stand mixer, adding the salt and about half the sugar and beating until well combined, about 2 minutes. Add the remaining sugar and beat until well mixed. Add the sour cream, lemon juice, zest, and vanilla and beat until the mixture is perfectly smooth. Separate 2 of the eggs and add the 2 egg yolks, with the mixer running. (You won't need the 2 whites.) Now break in the remaining 6 eggs, beating all the while.

3. BAKE THE CAKE. Place the springform pan with the cooked crust on a large baking sheet (to prevent spills). Pour the filling in and bake for 10 minutes at 500°F. Then, without opening the door, reduce the temperature of the oven to 225°F and bake until the top is golden brown and puffy and just barely trembles when you jiggle it, about 1¼ hours. Cool on a rack. The cake will fall a bit, but that's okay. Run a thin-bladed knife around the perimeter and remove the sides of the pan. Wrap the cake tightly in plastic and refrigerate. It keeps for up to 4 days.

4. SERVE THE CHEESECAKE. Let the cake stand at room temperature for about half an hour, then cut into thin wedges and serve with a dollop of preserves, if you wish. Cut with a serrated knife that you've dipped into hot water to make even cuts.

coconut marzipan cake

Chewy, golden, and tender, this cake needs no accompaniment. If you happen to have fresh berries on hand, however, a side of those is welcome. The hint of Bacardi coconut rum lifts the flavor into Caribbean heaven. And you can make swell summer drinks with the rest of the bottle.

baker's tip

Marzipan, or almond paste, comes in a tube and is sold in the baking section of the supermarket. You may have to give it a bit of encouragement to soften it enough to blend into the cake. A quick trip through the microwave will usually do it. If it still seems mulish and difficult, chop it finely before adding it to the cake batter.

¾ cup sweetened, flaked coconut, divided

7 ounces marzipan

1 cup (2 sticks) soft, unsalted butter

½ cup sugar

1 tablespoon coconut rum

6 large eggs

1 cup sifted cake flour

1 teaspoon baking powder

¼ teaspoon salt

BERRY TOPPING

3 cups fresh raspberries or other fruits

1 tablespoon confectioners' sugar

1. PREPARE TO BAKE. Preheat the oven to 400°F. Arrange the rack in the middle of the oven. Butter a 10-inch round springform pan and sprinkle ½ cup of the coconut on the bottom and sides. Soften the marzipan in the microwave for 20 to 30 seconds and crumble.

2. MAKE THE BATTER. Cream the marzipan and butter in a stand mixer until light, and then add the sugar and coconut rum. Beat until smooth. Break the eggs into the mixture, one at a time, beating well. Sift the flour, baking powder, and salt onto a piece of wax paper and then spoon it into the mixture. Beat just until the mixture is smooth. Use a light touch.

3. BAKE THE CAKE. Transfer the mixture to the prepared pan and sprinkle with the remaining ¼ cup coconut. Bake until the surface is golden brown and a wooden pick inserted into the center comes out clean, 20 to 25 minutes. Cool in the pan on a rack for 5 minutes. Run a thin-bladed knife around the edge, remove the sides of the pan, then hold a cake plate over the cake, flip it over, and remove the disk.

4. FINISH THE CAKE. While the cake is baking, toss the berries with the confectioners' sugar. Top the cake with the berries. Serve warm.

rhoda berman's banana sour cream cake with lemon glaze

Here's the answer for those two nearly black bananas on the countertop. Whip up this quick cake and serve it with a cup of tea. The crust is a glorious golden brown, and the crumb is fine, smooth, and speckled with tiny banana seeds. It simply radiates banana and lemon aromas. The glaze soaks in so that it becomes a part of the cake. You may use orange or tangerine instead of lemon if you prefer. It's also tempting with nothing but a dusting of confectioners' sugar.

baker's tip

Nothing works better than a common table fork for mashing bananas. Just peel them into a bowl and mash away. Don't worry about a few dark bits.

2 large eggs

1 cup sugar

½ cup (1 stick) unsalted butter, melted

1 cup mashed ripe banana (about 2 medium)

1½ teaspoons vanilla extract

¼ cup sour cream

1½ cups sifted cake flour

1 teaspoon baking powder

1 teaspoon baking soda

½ teaspoon salt

½ cup pecan pieces

LEMON GLAZE

¾ cup sifted confectioners' sugar

1 teaspoon grated lemon zest

5 tablespoons fresh lemon juice

1. **PREPARE TO BAKE.** Arrange the rack in the middle of the oven and preheat it to 400°F. Spritz a 9-by-2-inch shiny square pan with Baker's Joy. Warm the unbroken eggs in a bowl of hot tap water for about 5 minutes.

2. **MAKE THE BATTER.** Beat the eggs and sugar together in a stand mixer. Pour in the melted butter, and then add the banana, vanilla, and sour cream. Sift the flour, baking powder, baking soda, and salt onto a piece of wax paper, and then add to the butter mixture, a spoonful at a time. Stir in the nuts.

3. **BAKE THE CAKE.** Transfer the batter to the baking pan and bake until a toothpick comes out clean and the cake is brown and beginning to pull away from the sides, 25 to 30 minutes.

4. **FINISH THE CAKE.** Cool the cake in the pan on a rack for 10 minutes, then flip it out onto the rack to cool completely. To make the lemon glaze, combine the confectioners' sugar, lemon zest, and juice in the mixer and beat until smooth. Apply in a thin coat to the warm cake by drizzling it from a tablespoon, allowing some to run down the sides as well as to soak into the top. Serve warm, cut into squares.

sunshine génoise with
silky buttercream

This cake is pure velvet, as tender and golden as youth. Adding 12 egg yolks yields a rich, complex flavor and a fine, dense texture. Get organic eggs if you can, for the richest color and taste. Like all génoise, this one relies on a large amount of egg for its texture, but unlike others, it's so moist you needn't add syrup. It's a great party cake. The structure is secure. Slather it with buttercream, top with curls of citrus zest, fruits, nuts, or fresh or candied violets (see page 83), and it's a celebration.

baker's tip

This process calls for you to whisk the ingredients into egg yolks set over simmering water in a double boiler arrangement. Don't fret if you don't own one: simply improvise, using a metal bowl set over a pan of simmering water. Use a portable electric mixer or a balloon whisk to mix the batter. Vigorously whisk the egg yolks and continue until they form a thick ribbon.

To prevent crystallization of the sugar syrup when making the buttercream, use a heavy pan with a lip such as Le Creuset (see Mail-Order Sources, page 189). Cover the pan until the syrup comes to a boil, then uncover it and boil without stirring. Whisk it off the fire the instant it reaches the soft ball stage (238°F) and pour it in a thin stream into the beaten egg yolks, keeping the mixer on high speed. Try not to let the hot syrup hit the beaters, or it will spin the syrup onto the edges of the bowl instead of properly incorporating it.

12 large egg yolks

9 tablespoons unsalted butter

1 cup sifted cake flour

3 tablespoons cornstarch

½ teaspoon salt

1 teaspoon vanilla extract

¼ cup water

¾ cup plus 2 tablespoons sugar

1. **PREPARE TO BAKE.** Arrange the rack in the middle of the oven and preheat it to 400°F. Break the egg yolks into a metal bowl and place it over a larger pan of simmering water to warm the yolks, stirring periodically to prevent curdling. Spritz one 9-inch round springform pan or kugelhopf cake pan with Baker's Joy. Melt the butter in a small, heavy saucepan over medium heat and cook until the solids begin to brown. Remove from the heat to prevent burning.

2. **MAKE THE BATTER.** Sift the flour, cornstarch, and salt onto a piece of wax paper. Combine the vanilla with the water in a glass measure. Add the sugar to the egg yolks, a spoonful at a time, while beating them, still over simmering water, with a portable electric mixer set on high speed or a balloon whisk until tripled in volume, about 5 minutes. Stir in the water mixture. Sprinkle half the flour mixture over, and fold it in with the balloon whisk or a rubber spatula. Add the remaining flour and whisk it in just until the flour disappears. Fold in the melted butter just until incorporated.

continued

SILKY BUTTERCREAM

3 large egg yolks

½ cup sugar

¼ cup water

1 cup (2 sticks) soft, unsalted butter

2 tablespoons liqueur of your choice

Grated lemon zest, for sprinkling

3. BAKE THE CAKE. Transfer the batter to the prepared pan, smoothing the top with a spatula. Bake until golden brown and barely springing back at the touch, about 25 minutes. Cool on a rack in the pan for 5 minutes, then, if using a spring-form pan, run a thin-bladed knife around the edge and lift off the sides of the pan. For a kugelhopf pan, loosen the cake from the edges only. Cool. Transfer the cake, still on the metal disk, to a cake stand.

4. FINISH THE CAKE. While the cake is cooling, make the buttercream. Beat the egg yolks in a bowl with an electric mixer until light in color. Meanwhile, combine the sugar and water in a small saucepan and bring to a boil, stirring only to dissolve the sugar. Heat to the soft ball stage, 238°F. Quickly pour the syrup in a thin stream into the egg yolks, beating constantly until completely cool. Beat in the butter, adding it a pinch at a time, and any liqueur you wish. It's okay to frost a warm cake with this warm icing. Frost the sides and then the top, using an offset spatula. Make swirls in the top, and finish with a grating of lemon zest.

boston cream pie

MAKES ONE 9-INCH ROUND CAKE, TO SERVE 8

A Boston cream pie is nothing more than a rich, single-layer yellow cake split in half and then filled with pastry cream and finished with a chocolate glaze. If you can make the basic cake, you're nearly there. Add edible flowers and a sprig of mint for garnish if you wish.

baker's tip — For best results, cool the cake before slicing it in half. Cool the pastry cream before spreading it onto the cake. Once the cake is glazed, cover loosely and refrigerate.

Sunshine Génoise batter (page 81)

Pastry Cream (page 154)

CHOCOLATE GLAZE

6 ounces fine-quality bittersweet chocolate, broken into pieces

3 tablespoons water

2 tablespoons unsalted butter

1½ tablespoons light corn syrup

¼ teaspoon salt

Fresh edible flowers and mint leaves, for garnish

1. BAKE THE CAKE. Prepare and bake the génoise as directed in steps 1 through 3 of the Sunshine Génoise recipe. While it bakes, make the pastry cream. To make the glaze, in a metal bowl set over a saucepan of barely simmering water, melt the chocolate with the water, butter, corn syrup, and salt, stirring until smooth. Remove the bowl from the pan.

2. ASSEMBLE THE CAKE. Remove the cake from the pan, halve it horizontally with a long, serrated knife, and arrange the bottom half, cut side up, on a plate. Top the bottom half with the pastry cream, spreading it to the edge; put the remaining cake half, cut side down, on the pastry cream; and pour the glaze on top of it, spreading it to the edge and letting it drip down the side. The Boston cream pie may be made 1 day in advance and kept covered loosely and chilled. Garnish the cake with flowers and mint leaves.

how to make candied violets

2 large egg whites

Sugar, for dipping

1 large bunch wild violets, including stems

Preheat the oven to 200°F. Beat the egg whites just until frothy in a small bowl. Place some sugar in another bowl. Taking one violet at a time, pick it up by the stem and dip it into the egg white, covering all the surfaces. Gently dip it into the sugar, again being sure that all of the petals, top and bottom, are covered. Place on a baking sheet lined with wax or parchment paper. Using a toothpick, open the petals to their original shape. Sprinkle sugar on any uncoated areas. Dry in the oven for 30 to 40 minutes, or until the sugar crystallizes. Gently remove the violets to wire racks, using a spatula or two-tined fork. Sprinkle with sugar again if the violets appear syrupy. Cool. Store in an airtight tin with wax or parchment paper between the layers.

olive oil honey cake

Italians believe olive oil is good for everything. Taste this cake and you'll know they're right. The cake is tender, aromatic, and tangy with just a hint of lemon. Add a topping of seasonal berries and/or fruits and you have a quick, one-layer cake to adore.

baker's tip Because this cake is made with oil instead of butter or shortening, it requires careful spritzing with Baker's Joy in the pan so the cake has something to hang on to while it bakes.

3 large eggs

¾ cup mild honey

1½ cups extra virgin olive oil

1½ cups milk

2 teaspoons fresh lemon juice

Grated zest of 1 lime

2 cups sifted cake flour

1 teaspoon baking powder

1 teaspoon baking soda

½ teaspoon salt

Confectioners' sugar, for dusting

Fresh, seasonal fruit and berries, for serving

1. **PREPARE TO BAKE.** Arrange the rack in the middle of the oven and preheat it to 400°F. Spritz a 9-inch shiny round aluminum cake pan with Baker's Joy and set aside. Place the unbroken eggs in a bowl of hot water for about 5 minutes.

2. **MAKE THE BATTER.** Beat the honey and eggs together with an electric mixer, then add the oil, milk, lemon juice, and zest and mix well. Sift the flour, baking powder, baking soda, and salt onto a piece of wax paper. Spoon this into the honey mixture and stir until mixed.

3. **BAKE THE CAKE.** Pour the batter into the prepared pan and bake until a wooden pick comes out clean, about 35 minutes. Cool in the pan for 10 minutes, then flip the cake out onto the rack to cool completely.

4. **FINISH THE CAKE.** Dust with confectioners' sugar and serve with fruit and berries.

eggnog chocolate cake

You knew there was more than one use for eggnog, didn't you? Put it into this quick cake and you'll have something to serve alongside that holiday drink. It's festive, fast, and fun.

baker's tip

Seized chocolate is unforgettable. Instead of being silky, oozy, smooth, and compliant, it is grainy, rigid, and unresponsive. It cannot be remelted and must be thrown away. What causes chocolate to seize up? Too much heat!

1 tablespoon unsweetened Dutch process cocoa powder

2 ounces (2 squares) unsweetened chocolate

¼ cup (½ stick) soft, unsalted butter

1 cup best-quality eggnog

1 teaspoon vanilla extract

½ cup sugar

1 cup sifted cake flour

2 teaspoons baking powder

½ teaspoon ground nutmeg

Confectioners' sugar, for dusting (optional)

Whipped cream, for serving (optional)

1. **PREPARE TO BAKE.** Arrange a rack in the middle of the oven and preheat it to 400°F. Spritz an 8-inch square baking dish with Baker's Joy, then coat the pan with the cocoa powder. Combine the chocolate and butter in a microwave-safe bowl and melt in the microwave, about 1 minute. Stir to mix.

2. **MAKE THE BATTER.** Stir the eggnog, vanilla, and sugar together in a large bowl. Sift the flour, baking powder, and nutmeg onto a piece of wax paper, then spoon it into the batter and beat for 2 minutes with an electric mixer. Fold in the melted chocolate mixture.

3. **BAKE THE CAKE.** Pour the batter into the prepared pan and bake until a wooden pick comes out clean, 20 to 25 minutes. Cool in the pan on a rack. Turn out onto a cake plate.

4. **FINISH THE CAKE.** To serve, dust the cake with confectioners' sugar, or add a dollop of whipped cream, or just eat it plain with a glass of bourbon-laced eggnog dusted with nutmeg.

red, white, and blue
yogurt cake

Here's a Fourth of July cake. Take it to a picnic or serve it in the backyard. It's patriotic. It's a delicious, soft second cousin to a cheesecake.

baker's tip

To soften refrigerated or frozen butter or cream cheese, remove the foil wrapper, then place in the microwave and heat for 20 seconds on high. Squeeze gently to see if it's soft. Transfer to the mixer bowl and proceed.

3 large eggs, divided

½ cup (1 stick) soft, unsalted butter

4 ounces soft cream cheese

1 cup sugar, divided

1½ cups sifted cake flour

1½ teaspoons baking powder

4 cups fresh berries, including raspberries, blueberries, and perhaps sweet, pitted cherries

2 cups (16 ounces) vanilla-flavored yogurt

2 tablespoons cornstarch

1 tablespoon vanilla extract

1. PREPARE TO BAKE. Arrange the rack in the middle of the oven and preheat it to 400°F. Spritz a 10-inch springform pan with Baker's Joy. Place the unbroken eggs in a bowl of hot tap water for about 5 minutes.

2. MAKE THE BATTER. Add the butter, cream cheese, ½ cup of the sugar, 1 egg, flour, and baking powder in a large bowl. Stir with a wooden spoon to mix thoroughly, then pour into the prepared pan. Arrange the fruit on top. Rinse out the bowl, and add the yogurt, cornstarch, remaining ½ cup sugar, vanilla, and remaining 2 egg yolks. (You won't need the whites.) Whisk thoroughly, then spread on top of the cake.

3. BAKE THE CAKE. Bake until the crust is light brown around the edges and the middle is still a little jiggly, 30 to 35 minutes. Remove to a rack and cool thoroughly. Once the cake is cool, run a thin-bladed knife around the perimeter, and remove the sides of the pan. Serve at room temperature or chilled.

pecan cake with a peachy keen glaze

Using nuts for part of the flour is a tradition that harks back in time. Nut cakes not only taste good, they also keep well. Fannie Farmer first offered a recipe for a pecan cake in the 1918 edition of that cookbook. Of course, great pecans probably came from the tree in the backyard, and grandmama probably shucked and then ground the nuts in a mortar and pestle. Substitute your favorite nut for interesting cakes: walnuts, black walnuts, pistachios, filberts, or cashews. Each yields its own unique cake.

baker's tip

Your big job here is procurement. Buy top-quality pecans, and perfectly ripe, perfumed peaches, and you're on your way. How can you tell if peaches are ripe? Follow your nose. Stone fruits (peaches, apricots, nectarines, and plums) do not ripen after they're picked. If you can't smell their perfume from the end of the produce aisle, forget it. They were picked green and will never have any more flavor than a potato. In this case, choose frozen peaches, which were allowed to ripen on the tree and then quickly frozen. The flavor's locked in.

4 large eggs

⅔ cup pecan pieces

⅓ cup sifted cake flour

¼ teaspoon salt

⅔ cup sugar, divided

½ cup (1 stick) soft, unsalted butter

½ teaspoon vanilla extract

Grated zest of ½ lemon

1. **PREPARE TO BAKE.** Arrange the rack in the middle of the oven and preheat it to 400°F. Spritz a 9-inch shiny round aluminum cake pan with Baker's Joy. Warm the unbroken eggs in a bowl of hot tap water. Pulse the nuts 5 or 6 times in a food processor until they are dry and powdery. Toss with the flour on a piece of wax paper.

2. **MAKE THE BATTER.** Separate the eggs. Beat the whites with the salt until foamy, then turn the mixer speed to high and beat to stiff peaks, adding ⅓ cup of the sugar, a tablespoon at a time. Transfer to a second large bowl, and then, without washing the bowl, add the egg yolks to the mixer bowl with the remaining ⅓ cup sugar and beat until light. Beat in the butter, vanilla, and lemon zest until the mixture is smooth. Fold the yolk mixture into the beaten whites. Sprinkle the nut-flour mixture over the top and fold in.

PEACHY KEEN GLAZE

2 tablespoons soft, unsalted butter

½ cup mild honey

2 medium, ripe peaches, peeled, seeded, and chopped, or 1½ cups chopped frozen peaches

Juice and grated zest of ½ lemon

Best-quality vanilla ice cream, for serving

3. BAKE THE CAKE. Transfer the batter to the prepared pan and bake until golden and a wooden pick inserted in the middle comes out clean, 15 to 20 minutes. Cool the cake in the pan on a rack for 10 minutes, then run a thin-bladed knife around the edge and flip it onto a cake serving dish.

4. MAKE THE GLAZE. While the cake is cooling, make the glaze by melting the butter in a small saucepan and then adding the honey, peaches, and lemon juice and zest and boiling until thick and syrupy, 5 to 10 minutes. Pour over the warm cake just after placing it on the serving platter. Serve warm or at room temperature, with a scoop of vanilla ice cream.

spicy mexican chocolate cake

One blessed layer of airy-light spicy chocolate cake topped with Kahlúa whipped cream and a sprinkling of mango bits makes this a dessert to remember. If you have access to Mexican vanilla and Mexican chocolate (Ibarra), by all means use them. But the complexity of flavor that comes from this mixture of best-quality bittersweet chocolate, cinnamon, cayenne, coffee, and almonds is unforgettable. Viva Mexico!

baker's tip

Look for Ibarra chocolate in the Latin section of the supermarket, packed in a yellow hexagonal box. You'll note that this brand has a rich, granular texture and an intense chocolate taste. There is nothing quite like it in the American market. For best-quality, use Blue Cattle Truck Mexican Vanilla from Nutrition Lifestyles (see Mail-Order Sources, page 189).

3 large eggs

6 ounces best-quality bittersweet chocolate (or 2 discs Ibarra chocolate)

2 tablespoons brewed espresso coffee

⅓ cup roasted, salted almonds

½ cup sifted cake flour

¼ teaspoon salt

½ cup plus 2 tablespoons sugar, divided

½ cup (1 stick) soft, unsalted butter

½ teaspoon ground cinnamon

½ teaspoon cayenne pepper

½ teaspoon almond extract

1½ teaspoons vanilla extract (Mexican preferred)

1. PREPARE TO BAKE. Place the rack in the middle of the oven and preheat it to 400°F. Spritz an 8-inch shiny round aluminum cake pan or 6 ramekins with Baker's Joy. Place the unbroken eggs in a bowl of hot tap water. Combine the chocolate and coffee in a microwavable bowl and melt in the microwave, about 1 minute. Alternatively, heat on the stovetop in a small pan, stirring over low heat just until the chocolate begins to melt. Pulse the almonds in a food processor until powdery and dry. Sift and measure the flour. Toss the ground almonds and flour together in a small bowl. Separate the eggs.

2. MAKE THE BATTER. Beat the egg whites until foamy in a stand mixer, then add the salt and 2 tablespoons sugar and beat until stiff peaks form. Transfer to a second bowl. Without washing the mixer bowl, cream the butter until fluffy, then add the remaining ½ cup sugar, a tablespoon at a time. Mix for 1 minute, then add the egg yolks, one at a time, and beat until well mixed. Add the melted chocolate-coffee mixture, beating, and then add the cinnamon, cayenne, and almond and vanilla extracts, beating well. Fold in the beaten egg whites and sifted flour in thirds, alternately, just until blended.

continued

TOPPING

½ cup whipping cream

1 tablespoon Kahlúa

½ teaspoon vanilla extract

1 tablespoon sugar

1 mango, peeled and cut into bite-sized pieces

3. BAKE THE CAKE. Transfer the batter to the prepared cake pan and bake until a wooden pick comes out clean, 20 to 25 minutes. Cool in the pan on a rack for 5 minutes, running a thin-bladed knife around the perimeter. Flip over onto a serving dish.

4. FINISH THE CAKE. To make the topping, whip the cream with the Kahlúa, vanilla, and sugar. Cut the cake into wedges and top each with a dollop of whipped cream. Finish with the mango bits.

mocha fudge chip
pudding cake

Why do we love pudding cakes? No pan to grease, no egg whites to beat, no frosting to make. The pudding forms in the pan and makes a rich, decadent dessert that calls for a side of vanilla ice cream.

baker's tip

Wondering what Dutch process cocoa is and why you should choose it? Well, it's not from the land of tulips, for openers. It's a process whereby cocoa beans are alkalized to yield a darker powder with a stronger chocolate flavor. It also dissolves more easily in batters. And while Dutch process cocoa used to be hard to find and expensive, now even Hershey's makes one that is sold in grocery stores everywhere. But if you don't have it or don't like it, don't despair. Substitute unsweetened cocoa powder measure for measure in any recipe. You will get a lighter-colored chocolate result.

¼ cup (½ stick) soft, unsalted butter

2 teaspoons vanilla extract

½ cup half-and-half

1 cup sifted cake flour

2 teaspoons baking powder

1 cup sugar, divided

¼ teaspoon salt

½ cup unsweetened Dutch process cocoa powder, divided

1 cup (6 ounces) semisweet chocolate chips

1 cup chopped walnuts

¾ cup firmly packed dark brown sugar

1¾ cups freshly brewed espresso or other strong coffee

Vanilla ice cream, for serving

1. PREPARE TO BAKE. Preheat the oven to 400°F. Spritz a 9-inch square pan with Baker's Joy. In a glass measure, melt the butter in the microwave on high, about 45 seconds, then add the vanilla and half-and-half. Stir.

2. MAKE THE BATTER. Sift the flour, baking powder, ¾ cup of the sugar, salt, and ¼ cup of the cocoa powder into a bowl. Toss in the chocolate chips and walnuts. Pour in the butter mixture. Mix well with a rubber spatula. Spread the mixture into the prepared pan. Combine the brown sugar and the remaining ¼ cup sugar and ¼ cup cocoa in a small bowl. The mixture will be lumpy; that's okay. Sprinkle on top of the cake batter. Pour the hot coffee over this.

3. BAKE THE CAKE. Bake until the top is set and the bottom mixture is bubbly, about 20 minutes. Serve warm with vanilla ice cream.

über-chocolate cake

If chocolate is your weakness, this flourless cake's for you: dense, dark, and mysterious. Cocoa stands in for flour and gives the cake great structure. Careful baking will yield a nearly black confection with an oozing, molten center. Use a stand mixer to beat the eggs, and a candy thermometer to watch the sugar syrup reach 220°F. Choose the best grade of chocolate you can lay your hands on. After 15 minutes of baking, open the door and jiggle the cake. It is done when it almost quits jiggling and a toothpick yields just a hint of that molten center. Don't overbake.

baker's tip

Unfortunately, the old saw, "you get what you pay for" applies here. The best cocoa, Droste, and the best chocolate, Valrhona, do cost more, but they're worth it. If you can't find those brands, simply rely on top-quality imported Swiss or Belgian chocolate and Dutch process cocoa. When making the sugar syrup, use a saucepan with a lip such as Le Creuset (see Mail-Order Sources, page 189) so you can pour it into the beaten egg easily.

1½ cups plus 1 tablespoon best-quality unsweetened Dutch process cocoa powder, divided

6 large eggs

1⅓ cups sugar, divided

⅛ teaspoon salt

1 teaspoon vanilla extract

½ cup water

4 ounces (⅔ cup) best-quality bittersweet chocolate, broken into pieces

1½ cups (3 sticks) soft, unsalted butter

Whipped cream, for serving

Raspberries, for serving

1. PREPARE TO BAKE. Arrange the rack in the middle of the oven and preheat it to 400°F. Spritz an 8-inch shiny round aluminum cake pan with Baker's Joy, then dust the bottom with 1 tablespoon of the cocoa powder. Place the unbroken eggs in a bowl of hot tap water for about 5 minutes.

2. MAKE THE BATTER. Combine the eggs and ⅓ cup of the sugar in the large bowl of a stand mixer. Add the salt and vanilla. Beat on high while you prepare the sugar syrup.

Combine the water with the remaining 1 cup sugar in a heavy saucepan and boil until a candy thermometer reaches 220°F, about 4 minutes.

Remove the pan from the heat immediately, then stir in the 1½ cups cocoa powder and chocolate pieces until they are melted and smooth. Pinch off pieces of soft butter with your fingers and drop them into the chocolate mixture, stirring vigorously.

Turn the mixer down to low speed and pour the chocolate mixture into the eggs. Don't overwork it here. Turn the mixer off the second the chocolate is incorporated.

3. BAKE THE CAKE. Quickly scrape the mixture into the prepared cake pan. Bake until a wooden pick inserted in the middle comes out almost clean, with only a hint of an oozing, melting center, 15 to 20 minutes. Remove the cake from the oven. Let it cool in the pan on a rack for about 5 minutes. Run a thin-bladed knife around the perimeter, then turn it out onto a serving platter. Serve warm or at room temperature. Garnish with whipped cream and fresh raspberries.

sacher torte

Keep this in mind: The Sacher torte was invented by a 16-year-old baker's apprentice of the same name who was under the gun when the head baker got sick and his master demanded a cake to please his fussy, spoiled royal guests.

The Viennese kid came through and invented what is arguably the world's most famous cake. If a baker's apprentice could whip this up in 1832 without the benefit of electricity, mixers, or a reliable oven, why can't you?

I've pared down the method, using every tool in my arsenal, and now the recipe is yours with which to make your reputation. While the classic Sacher torte depends on best-quality European bittersweet chocolate offset by subtle apricot jam, you can make any changes that please you. Why not raspberry jam? Or orange marmalade? But remember, the basic recipe is, quite certainly, a piece of cake.

baker's tip
For a fantastic finish, whip some unsweetened heavy cream. I like to add a touch of Bacardi Ocho (the 8-year-old rum). Add just a dollop of the whipped cream to each serving. Pure pleasure.

6 large eggs

½ cup sugar, divided

½ cup (1 stick) soft, unsalted butter

4 ounces best-quality bittersweet chocolate

1 tablespoon water

1 tablespoon golden rum (try Bacardi Ocho)

½ cup sifted cake flour

3 tablespoons apricot preserves or other all-fruit preserves

½ cup unsweetened whipped cream, for serving (with maybe a touch of rum to flavor it)

1. PREPARE TO BAKE. Arrange the rack in the middle of the oven and preheat it to 400°F. Spritz an 8-inch shiny round aluminum cake pan with Baker's Joy. Place the unbroken eggs into a bowl of hot tap water for 5 minutes before separating.

2. MAKE THE BATTER. Separate the eggs into small bowls, transferring the whites to the large bowl of your stand mixer. Beat the egg whites on high speed until foamy, then add 2 tablespoons of the sugar and beat until stiff peaks form. Transfer the beaten egg whites to another bowl. No need to wash the beaters and bowl. Add the soft butter and remaining sugar to the bowl and beat on high until light. Meanwhile, place the chocolate and water in a microwavable dish and melt the chocolate, about 1 minute on high. Stir the rum into the chocolate mixture and whisk in the egg yolks, then spoon it into the butter-sugar mixture, beating well. Turn off the mixer. Fold the beaten egg whites into the mixture, then sprinkle the flour over the top and barely fold it in.

BITTERSWEET CHOCOLATE FROSTING

4 ounces bittersweet chocolate (the other half of that best-quality chocolate bar you bought just for this purpose)

2 tablespoons sugar

¼ cup water

1 tablespoon unsalted butter

3. BAKE THE CAKE. Transfer the batter to the baking pan and bake until a wooden pick comes out clean, 20 to 25 minutes. Cool the cake in the pan on a rack for about 5 minutes, or until it begins to pull away from the sides. Flip the cake onto a cake plate and let cool. Warm the apricot preserves in the microwave for about 20 seconds and spread a thin layer over the cake. Continue to cool it in the refrigerator, uncovered.

4. MAKE THE FROSTING. Once the cake is cool, make the frosting. Using a 2-cup glass measure, melt the chocolate, sugar, and water in the microwave, about 2 minutes on high, then whisk in the butter to make a smooth icing. Pour the mixture onto the top and sides of the cake and smooth with an offset spatula. Return to the refrigerator so it can set up. Serve the cake with a dollop of unsweetened whipped cream. Store for 2 days under a cake bell.

chocolate almond queen of sheba

Julia Child introduced this fine French cake made with almond flour to Americans long before the advent of food processors and microwaves. What was once labor intensive is now easy enough to become a staple in any kitchen and a sentimental favorite for birthdays.

baker's tip When making your own almond flour, take care not to overprocess the almonds or you'll release the natural oils in the nuts and the mixture will begin to clump. Simply pulse the processor a few times until the blanched almonds are reduced to a powdery, dry flour.

1 tablespoon unsweetened Dutch process cocoa powder

3 large eggs

3 ounces bittersweet chocolate

1 ounce (1 square) unsweetened chocolate

2 tablespoons espresso or dark rum

⅓ cup blanched almonds

½ teaspoon almond extract

1 tablespoon lemon juice

½ teaspoon cream of tartar

¼ teaspoon salt

½ cup sugar, divided

½ cup sifted cake flour

¼ cup (½ stick) unsalted butter

Confectioners' sugar, for dusting

Fresh raspberries, for serving

1. PREPARE TO BAKE. Arrange the rack in the middle of the oven and preheat it to 400°F. Spritz a 9-inch shiny round aluminum cake pan with Baker's Joy. Sprinkle the bottom with the cocoa powder. Place the unbroken eggs in a bowl of hot tap water. Combine the unsweetened and bittersweet chocolates and espresso or rum in a glass measure and melt in the microwave on high, about 1 minute. Stir to mix. Pulse the almonds in a food processor until dry and powdery. Sprinkle with the almond extract. Set aside.

2. MAKE THE BATTER. Separate the eggs and whip the egg whites in a stand mixer until foamy, then add the lemon juice, cream of tartar, and salt and whip until soft peaks form. Sprinkle in 2 tablespoons of the sugar and beat until shiny, tall peaks form. Transfer to a second bowl. No need to wash the beaters and bowl. Toss the flour with the pulverized almonds on a sheet of wax paper.

In the mixer bowl, cream the butter and remaining sugar until light, and then add the egg yolks, one at a time, beating thoroughly. Stir the melted chocolate until smooth, and then blend it into the egg yolk mixture. Fold the almond-flour mixture into the egg whites in thirds, alternately with the chocolate-egg mixture. Do not overmix.

3. BAKE THE CAKE. Transfer the batter to the prepared pan and bake until a wooden pick inserted into the cake 2 inches from the side comes out clean, 12 to 15 minutes. The center should still be jiggly. Cool in the pan on a rack for 10 minutes, then flip it out to cool on the rack.

4. FINISH THE CAKE. For a fine finish, arrange a paper doily over the top of the cake and sprinkle with confectioners' sugar tapped through a strainer. Carefully lift away the paper to reveal the design. Nestle fresh raspberries on top of the cake and around the edges in clusters. Serve warm or cool.

torta cioccolata con crema y fragole

Here's one Italian grandmother's idea of a little plain cake. Black as death, egg-free, sweet and bitter all at once, this one-layer cake is as dramatic as opera. The top glistens and crunches with crystals. Who needs frosting?

baker's tip

Perfect Whipped Cream is cream whipped with a little sour cream for stability. Once you learn to make it, you may find yourself substituting it every time a recipe calls for whipped cream. The taste is sweet and tangy all at once. The texture is as sturdy as shaving cream, and the cream lasts in the refrigerator for up to 5 days.

⅓ cup plus 1 tablespoon Dutch process cocoa powder, divided

1½ cups sifted cake flour

1 teaspoon baking soda

1 cup sugar

½ teaspoon salt

1 cup brewed espresso

5 tablespoons olive oil

1½ teaspoons vanilla extract

1 tablespoon balsamic vinegar

PERFECT WHIPPED CREAM

1 cup whipping cream

2 tablespoons sour cream or crème fraîche

2 tablespoons sugar

1 teaspoon vanilla extract

Fresh raspberries, for serving

1. PREPARE TO BAKE. Arrange the rack in the middle of the oven and preheat it to 400°F. Spritz a 9-inch shiny round aluminum cake pan with Baker's Joy, then dust it lightly with 1 tablespoon of the cocoa powder.

2. MAKE THE BATTER. Whisk the flour, the remaining ⅓ cup cocoa powder, baking soda, sugar, and salt together in a large bowl. Stir together the coffee, oil, vanilla, and vinegar in a 2-cup glass measure. Whisk into the dry ingredients, blending just until it's lump free.

3. BAKE THE CAKE. Pour the batter into the prepared pan and bake until the top springs back at the touch and a wooden pick comes out clean, 20 to 25 minutes.

4. FINISH THE CAKE. Cool the cake in the pan on a rack. Turn it out onto a cake plate. To make Perfect Whipped Cream, combine the whipping cream, sour cream, sugar, and vanilla and whip until soft peaks form. Refrigerate, covered, until time to serve. Top wedges of cake with Perfect Whipped Cream and a raspberry.

great cocoa

According to a *New York Times* taste test, all unsweetened cocoa powders are not created equal. Here is how the *Times* ranked cocoas, from the best to the worst.

1. Fauchon
2. Valrhona
3. Master's Choice Premium
4. La Maison du Chocolat
5. Droste Dutch Process
6. Dean & DeLuca Bensdorp Cocoa
7. Schokinag Christopher Norman
8. Green & Black's Fairtrade Organic Cocoa
9. Scharffen Berger Natural Cocoa Powder
10. Nestlé Toll House Baking Cocoa
11. Ghirardelli Unsweetened Cocoa
12. Saco Premium Cocoa
13. Chatfield's Premium Cocoa Powder
14. Hershey's Cocoa
15. Ah!Laska Unsweetened Baker's Cocoa, certified organic

4

Cupcakes and Baby
CAKES

In New York City, at both Magnolia Bakery and the Cup Cake Café, hungry cupcake lovers line up to choose from the just-made gems. They're perfect for peripatetic street munchers on their way to and from work. But when a New York caterer served miniature wedding cakes, aka cupcakes, at a fancy East Hampton wedding, we knew these little jewels had arrived. And why not? They're quick, they're easy if you use paper liners, and they are portable. They're also popular with kids from 3 to 93.

A properly made cupcake looks much like a muffin, with its characteristic mushroom head extending just barely beyond the circumference of the cylinder. Sometimes, if you are planning to frost or glaze the cakes, however, you may not want that big top. For those cakes, it's better to fill the cups less full so that you have a gently rounded top to hold more frosting.

Shiny aluminum cupcake pans heat up quickly and cool down quickly so that your cakes come up and stay up when baked in this manner. I always recommend paper liners for cupcakes. If portability is your goal, line muffin tins with traditional paper liners—plain or fancy. If you'd like to *bake* in paper cups without the metal pan, order from Kitchen Conservatory (see Mail-Order Sources, page 189). This company also sells paper baking cups for loaf cakes as well as paper liners and display materials for cakes. These papers will yield architecturally-sided cakes.

You can get as fancy as you want to when finishing these little jewels. If you are good with a pastry bag and fancy tips, now's your chance to shine. If you prefer a simple frosting that you can dunk the heads of your cakes in, that's fine too. As for me, the plain, well-flavored cake often stands alone, with no frosting at all. It all just depends upon your temperament and your desires. You'll find the recipes in this chapter easy going. No fancy footwork here, just great taste and simple finishes.

For cool colors to tint the frosting, order from the Wilton Store (see Mail-Order Sources, page 189). There you'll find not only the usual primary colors, but also a number of different palettes to choose from: pastel, garden, and extra-szooschy colors. Make our simple decorating icing (see page 109), color it to suit, and you're on your way to sizzling, gorgeous cupcakes.

blueberry cupcakes

How do these cupcakes differ from blueberry muffins? Let's be frank here. A muffin is often a cupcake in disguise, so why not call a spade a spade? They're cakes. They're achingly tender with tiny explosions of fresh blueberry flavor. And they're nestled under a sweet/sour cream cheese frosting that gives them an edge over any so-called muffins.

baker's tip 〉 If using frozen blueberries, drain them in a colander before folding them into the batter, taking care not to break them down by overmixing.

2 large eggs

½ cup (1 stick) soft, unsalted butter

1 cup sugar

1½ cups sifted cake flour

1 teaspoon baking powder

½ teaspoon salt

½ cup milk

1 cup fresh or frozen blueberries

1 teaspoon vanilla extract

CREAM CHEESE FROSTING

4 ounces soft cream cheese

¼ cup (½ stick) soft, unsalted butter

2 cups sifted confectioners' sugar

¼ teaspoon salt

3 tablespoons milk

½ teaspoon vanilla extract

1. **PREPARE TO BAKE.** Arrange the rack in the middle of the oven and preheat it to 400°F. Line 12 standard muffin cups with paper liners. Place the eggs in a bowl of hot tap water.

2. **MAKE THE BATTER.** Cream the butter and sugar until light, about 3 minutes in a stand mixer. Sift the flour, baking powder, and salt onto a piece of wax paper, and then add to the butter mixture in thirds, alternately with the milk. Toss the blueberries with the vanilla, and then fold into the mixture.

3. **BAKE THE CAKES.** Divide the batter among the muffin cups, about ⅓ cup each, and bake until a wooden pick inserted into the center comes out clean, 12 to 15 minutes. Cool on a rack.

4. **FROST THE CAKES.** While the cakes are baking, make the frosting. Beat the cream cheese and butter together until light, then add the confectioners' sugar, salt, milk, and vanilla and beat until smooth and thick, adding additional milk as needed. Dip the cupcakes into the frosting and twist to swirl the frosting.

lemon-glazed vanilla pansy cakes

What a great way to welcome spring then with simple golden vanilla cupcakes, glazed with lemon and then finished with pansies or other edible flowers. When somebody asked me to throw an impromptu bridal shower, this is what I served. Lovely to look at, puckery sweet in the mouth.

baker's tip

The idea of a citrus glaze is as wide as it is deep. Freely substitute among orange, blood orange, tangerine, clementine, or grapefruit for the zesty glaze. Just measure, strain, and go forth. Cluster the finished cakes on a large platter for an edible posy.

4 large eggs
1 cup (2 sticks) soft, unsalted butter
1½ cups sugar
¼ cup milk
1 teaspoon vanilla extract
2 cups sifted cake flour
1 teaspoon baking powder
½ teaspoon salt

LEMON GLAZE
¼ cup fresh lemon juice
Grated zest of ½ lemon
1½ cups sugar

18 edible flowers, such as pansies or roses (see what's for sale at the organic market)

1. PREPARE TO BAKE. Arrange the rack in the middle of the oven and preheat it to 400°F. Line 18 standard muffin cups with paper liners. Place the unbroken eggs in a bowl of hot tap water.

2. MAKE THE BATTER. Cream the butter and sugar in a large mixer bowl until light, 2 minutes. With the mixer running, add the eggs, one at a time, then add the milk and vanilla. Spoon the flour, baking powder, and salt into the batter and mix for 2 minutes.

3. BAKE THE CAKES. Divide the batter among the muffin cups, about ⅓ cup each, and bake until a wooden pick comes out clean, 10 to 12 minutes. Cool in the pan on a rack for 5 minutes, and then remove the cupcakes to the rack to cool.

4. MAKE THE GLAZE. While the cakes are baking, combine the lemon juice, zest, and sugar in a small saucepan and cook, covered, over medium heat, stirring until transparent, about 10 minutes. Test to see if the syrup forms a "string" when dropped from a spoon. When it does, take it off the heat. Spoon the hot glaze over the cupcakes as soon as they come out of the oven. Top each cake with a small nontoxic, organic (pesticide-free) pansy, rose, scented geranium leaf, or other edible flower.

orange blossom vanilla baby cakes

Featured at a tony East Hampton wedding, these adorable little cakes were passed on a tray to wedding guests. Made in gold foil papers, each pure white cake was dunked into sumptuous orange-perfumed buttercream.

baker's tip *If you want a pure white cake, use shortening. If you want a more flavorful cake, opt for butter. What to do with all those lovely egg yolks? Make pastry cream (see page 154). You can serve it alongside the cakes, or you can split them and make a lovely cream center.*

4 large eggs

2½ cups sifted cake flour

1½ cups sugar

1 teaspoon baking powder

1 teaspoon salt

½ teaspoon baking soda

1 cup sour cream

¼ cup water

¾ cup (1½ sticks) soft, unsalted butter or vegetable shortening

1 teaspoon vanilla extract

1 teaspoon almond extract

ORANGE BLOSSOM FROSTING

1 cup granulated sugar

1 tablespoon light corn syrup

⅛ teaspoon cream of tartar

½ cup water

2 large egg whites

¼ cup sifted confectioners' sugar

1 tablespoon fresh orange juice

1 tablespoon grated orange zest

1 teaspoon vanilla extract

Julienned orange zest and edible green leaves, for garnish

1. **PREPARE TO BAKE.** Arrange the rack in the middle of the oven and preheat it to 400°F. Place paper liners in 24 standard muffin cups or 12 large Texas-size muffin cups. Place the unbroken eggs in a bowl of hot tap water.

2. **MAKE THE BATTER.** Sift the flour, sugar, baking powder, salt, and baking soda into a stand mixer bowl. Add the sour cream, water, and butter and beat for 2 minutes. Separate the eggs and add the unbeaten egg whites, vanilla, and almond extract. Beat for 2 minutes, scraping the sides of the bowl as needed.

3. **BAKE THE CAKES.** Add about ⅓ cup batter to each muffin cup (double it for the larger cups). Bake until golden on top and until a wooden pick inserted in the center comes out clean, 15 to 20 minutes. Cool on a rack completely before frosting.

4. **MAKE THE FROSTING.** While the cakes cool, combine the granulated sugar, corn syrup, cream of tartar, and water in a small, heavy saucepan with a lip, such as Le Creuset. Cover and cook for 3 minutes, or until the steam has washed down any sugar crystals on the side of the pan. Uncover and cook until a candy thermometer reads 238°F. While the syrup cooks, beat the egg whites until stiff; then, with the motor running, pour in the hot syrup. Beat for 10 minutes, and then add the confectioners' sugar, orange juice and zest, and vanilla. Beat until the mixture is thick and shiny. Dip the cooled cakes in the frosting. Decorate each cake with additional strips of orange zest and a shiny green leaf.

decorating icing

Easy as can be and limited only by your notions of color theory, here's the basic icing to make for decorating these and all other cakes. For cool colors, order from the Wilton Store (see Mail-Order Sources, page 189). This icing can be used in a pastry bag with fancy tips, or it can be used to top cupcakes. To spread it, you may wish to add a teaspoon or more of water. Use your judgment here. This is frosting that mostly looks good. Think of it as an art medium, and go forth.

1 pound (1 box) confectioners' sugar

4 teaspoons powdered egg whites (such as Just Whites or Wilton)

⅓ cup water

1 tablespoon fresh lemon juice

1 teaspoon vanilla extract

Food coloring, for tinting

1. MAKE THE FROSTING. Beat all of the ingredients except the food coloring together in a stand mixer at medium speed just until combined, then raise the speed to high and continue beating until the frosting holds stiff peaks, scraping down the sides of the bowl as needed, about 3 minutes.

2. COLOR THE FROSTING. Divide the frosting among 3 or 4 bowls and tint it by adding drops of food coloring. Stir with a fork. Cover with plastic wrap, letting the plastic fit down tight against the frosting, then refrigerate until ready to use.

red raspberry christmas candle cakes

Any December birthday kids on your list? Try these. Each little cake, spicy, fruity, and sweet, nestles under a snow-white cap of frosting and is decorated with a red or green sugar-frosted jelly wreath and a bright red birthday candle.

baker's tip { Use all-fruit raspberry preserves for the most punched-up flavor, but try strawberry or other all-fruit preserves according to your own taste. Don't choose regular preserves, which have too much sugar and not enough fruit to provide the flavor hit you're looking for.

2 large eggs

½ cup (1 stick) soft, unsalted butter

1 cup sugar

1¾ cups sifted cake flour

½ teaspoon baking soda

½ teaspoon salt

1 teaspoon ground cinnamon

½ teaspoon ground cloves

½ teaspoon ground allspice

½ teaspoon ground nutmeg

½ cup buttermilk

½ cup all-fruit raspberry jam

½ cup chopped pecans

WHITE FROSTING

1 cup sifted confectioners' sugar

¼ cup (½ stick) soft, unsalted butter

⅛ teaspoon salt

2 tablespoons milk

12 red and green sugar-coated jelly wreaths, for decoration

12 red birthday candles

1. PREPARE TO BAKE. Arrange the rack in the middle of the oven and preheat it to 400°F. Line 12 standard muffin cups with paper liners. Place the eggs in a bowl of hot tap water.

2. MAKE THE BATTER. Beat the butter until fluffy, then spoon in the sugar and continue to cream until light. Break the eggs in one at a time and beat. Sift the flour, baking soda, salt, cinnamon, cloves, allspice, and nutmeg onto a piece of wax paper, and then add to the butter mixture in thirds, alternately with the buttermilk. Fold in the jam and nuts.

3. BAKE THE CAKES. Divide the batter among the muffin cups, about ⅓ cup each, and bake until a toothpick comes out clean, 12 to 15 minutes.

4. FINISH THE CAKES. While the cakes cool, whisk the confectioners' sugar, butter, salt, and milk to make a pourable frosting. Frost each cake, and then decorate with a red or green jelly wreath. Place a red candle in the middle of each cake. Store under a glass bell.

ginger lemon cupcakes

These tender, dark, complicated, and moist cupcakes make a bed for a cloud of white icing studded with crystallized ginger. These are cupcakes for grownups. They'd make a wonderful groom's cake and are especially welcome in the winter.

baker's tip

Chop the crystallized ginger for the icing on a board, using a long chef's knife. Scrape it into a pile and chop again and again until you have pieces the size of peas.

1 large egg

½ cup (1 stick) unsalted butter

½ cup sugar

2½ cups sifted cake flour

1½ teaspoons baking soda

1 teaspoon ground cinnamon

1 teaspoon ground ginger

½ teaspoon ground cloves

½ teaspoon salt

½ cup dark molasses

½ cup full-flavored honey

½ cup water

½ cup lemon juice

Grated zest of 1 lemon

1. PREPARE TO BAKE. Line 12 standard muffin cups or 6 Texas-size muffin cups with paper liners. Arrange the rack in the middle of the oven and preheat it to 400°F. Place the unbroken egg in a bowl of hot tap water.

2. MAKE THE BATTER. Melt the butter in the microwave in a glass measure, then pour it into a stand mixer bowl along with the sugar and egg. Beat until light, about 3 minutes. Meanwhile, sift the flour, baking soda, cinnamon, ginger, cloves, and salt onto a piece of wax paper. Stir the molasses, honey, water, lemon juice, and zest into the glass measure. Add the flour mixture and the molasses mixture to the butter mixture, alternately in thirds, beating just until blended.

3. BAKE THE CAKES. Divide the batter among the muffin tins and bake until a wooden pick comes out clean, 15 to 20 minutes. Cool on a rack.

continued

CRYSTALLIZED GINGER ICING

1 cup sugar

½ cup water

2 large egg whites

⅛ teaspoon salt

⅛ teaspoon cream of tartar

1 teaspoon vanilla extract

½ cup finely chopped crystallized ginger

Grated lemon zest, for sprinkling

4. FINISH THE CAKES. While the cakes are baking, make the icing. Combine the sugar and water in a saucepan with a lip and bring to a boil. Cover and cook for 3 minutes or until steam has washed down all the sugar crystals, then uncover and cook to 238°F on a candy thermometer (the soft ball stage). While the sugar syrup is boiling, beat the egg whites at high speed until soft peaks form, then add the salt and cream of tartar and beat until stiff. Slowly pour the hot syrup into the egg whites while beating. Continue beating until soft peaks form, about 3 minutes, and then fold in the crystallized ginger. Dip the cakes into this icing. Sprinkle with grated lemon zest. Refrigerate until ready to serve. These cupcakes are best if served the day they're made.

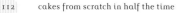

spicy corn cupcakes

Here's a great autumn cupcake. Serve it after a warm, satisfying soup supper, or with a cup of tea. The hint of spice will tease out the sweetness and earthiness of the corn.

baker's tip

It pays to take the extra step to toast nuts. Their complex flavors will leap to the forefront when toasted. But there's a fine line between toasted and burned nuts. It won't take you long to toast them, but you've got to keep your eye on the skillet and use your good nose and eyes to judge their readiness. Simply preheat a small skillet over medium heat, then add the pecan pieces and shake them until their fragrance runs up your nose and you notice golden, toasty spots forming. Immediately transfer them to a cool container so they don't burn.

3 large eggs

1 cup sifted cake flour

1½ teaspoons baking powder

⅓ cup yellow cornmeal

½ teaspoon salt

1 teaspoon ancho chile powder

¼ cup (½ stick) soft, unsalted butter

1 cup sugar

½ cup sour cream

CREAM CHEESE FROSTING

4 ounces soft cream cheese

¼ cup (½ stick) soft, unsalted butter

2 tablespoons sugar

½ teaspoon ancho chile powder

½ teaspoon vanilla extract

2 teaspoons whipping cream, or as needed

½ cup toasted, chopped pecans

1. **PREPARE TO BAKE.** Arrange the rack in the middle of the oven and preheat it to 400°F. Line a 12-cup standard muffin tin with paper liners. Place the unbroken eggs in a bowl of hot tap water.

2. **MAKE THE BATTER.** Sift the flour and baking powder into a bowl. Stir in the cornmeal, salt, and chile powder. Set aside. Cream the butter and sugar in a stand mixer until light. Add the eggs, one at a time, beating after each. Add the flour mixture in thirds, alternately with the sour cream, beginning and ending with the flour. Beat just until blended. Don't overdo it.

3. **BAKE THE CAKES.** Add ⅓ cup batter to each paper-lined muffin cup. Bake until a wooden pick inserted in the center comes out clean, 12 to 15 minutes. Cool on a rack.

4. **FROST THE CUPCAKES.** Beat the cream cheese in a medium bowl until smooth. Add the butter, sugar, ancho chile powder, and vanilla and beat again. Add enough cream to make a smooth paste. Finally, fold in the pecans. Once the cakes are cool, frost them. Store in an airtight tin.

baby fruitcakes

Why didn't somebody think of this sooner? A Texas bed-and-breakfast offers these mini-fruitcakes to guests with afternoon tea. You know how it is. A small serving of fruitcake is all anybody wants anyway. For holiday gifts, wrap them in cellophane with a gay, bright ribbon. Sweets to the sweet.

baker's tip

The big idea here is to use a certain volume of fruit and nuts—in this case, a total of 3¼ cups. If there is some particular fruit you don't like, substitute one of the others on the list, or your particular favorite. Just see to it that you wind up with the right volume in the cakes. Toss the fruits lightly with flour before folding them into the batter so they stay suspended in the batter and don't fall like stones to the bottom of the cakes.

3 large eggs

1 cup finely chopped mixed candied fruit

½ cup dried currants

½ cup sweetened, flaked coconut

¼ cup pitted, chopped dates

1 tablespoon lemon juice

Grated zest of ½ lemon

1 cup sifted cake flour, divided

¾ teaspoon baking powder

½ teaspoon salt

½ cup (1 stick) soft, unsalted butter

½ cup sugar

1 teaspoon vanilla extract

⅓ cup pineapple juice

1 cup pecan halves

1. PREPARE TO BAKE. Arrange a pan of water on the bottom rack of the oven. Arrange the top rack in the middle of the oven and preheat it to 400°F. Line 24 standard muffin cups with paper liners and spritz them with Baker's Joy. Place the eggs in a bowl of hot tap water.

2. MAKE THE BATTER. In a medium bowl, stir together the candied fruits, currants, coconut, and dates. Sprinkle with the lemon juice and zest and stir again. Toss with ¼ cup of the flour. Sift the remaining flour, baking powder, and salt onto a piece of wax paper. Cream the butter and sugar in a stand mixer until light. Add the eggs, one at a time, beating after each addition. Add the flour mixture to the butter mixture in thirds, alternately with the vanilla and pineapple juice. Fold in the fruit and nuts.

3. BAKE THE CAKES. Fill the paper-lined muffin cups almost to the top. Bake until a wooden pick comes out clean and the cakes are done, 15 to 20 minutes. Remove to a rack and prick 3 or 4 holes in each cake with a wooden skewer.

continued

RUM GLAZE

¼ cup sugar

¼ cup pineapple juice

1 tablespoon golden rum, such as Bacardi Ocho

1 teaspoon lemon juice

Grated zest of ½ lemon

Candied fruit and nuts, for decoration

4. FINISH THE CAKES. While the cakes are baking, make the glaze by bringing the sugar, pineapple juice, rum, lemon juice, and zest to a boil in a small saucepan. Spoon half the glaze over the warm cakes, slowly letting it soak in. Decorate with additional candied fruits and nuts.

peanut butter cupcakes with chocolate ganache

If you like peanut butter cookies, you'll like these cupcakes. Tender, aromatic, and peanutty, their flavor is only enhanced by a smooth cap of chocolate ganache studded with chopped salted peanuts. A birthday party delight, these cakes are perfect with their old-fashioned gooey icing.

baker's tip } Smooth peanut butter yields a fine, even crumb, but chunky peanut butter will give a crunchy texture as well as taste. It's your choice.

1 large egg

½ cup smooth peanut butter

¼ cup (½ stick) soft, unsalted butter

½ cup firmly packed dark brown sugar

1¼ cups sifted cake flour

1½ teaspoons baking powder

¼ teaspoon salt

⅔ cup whole milk

1 teaspoon vanilla extract

CHOCOLATE GANACHE

⅓ cup whipping cream

4 ounces bittersweet chocolate, chopped

⅓ cup salted peanuts, chopped

1. PREPARE TO BAKE. Arrange a rack in the middle of the oven and preheat it to 400°F. Line 12 standard muffin cups with paper liners and spritz with Baker's Joy. Place the unbroken egg in a bowl of hot tap water.

2. MAKE THE BATTER. Cream the peanut butter and butter until light, then add the sugar and continue to beat for about 3 minutes. Add the egg, beating. Meanwhile, sift the flour, baking powder, and salt onto a sheet of wax paper. Spoon in the flour, in thirds, alternately with the milk and vanilla. Mix just until the batter is smooth.

3. BAKE THE CAKES. Divide the batter among the muffin cups, about ⅓ cup each. Bake until the cakes are pale gold and a wooden pick comes out clean, 15 to 20 minutes. Cool on a rack.

4. MAKE THE FROSTING. While the cakes are baking, make the frosting. Place the cream in a 2-cup glass measure and heat to boiling in the microwave on high, about 1 minute, then add the chocolate and microwave on high for about 1½ minutes more. Let it stand for a few moments, then whisk until thick and glossy. Spread onto the cupcakes, using about 1 heaping teaspoon per cake, and then sprinkle with the chopped peanuts.

black bottom cupcakes

The basic cake batter in the bottom of these irresistible cakes is dark as night and has just exactly the right amount of sweetness. A dollop of tangy cream cheese filler with chocolate chips and chopped pecans mixed in makes these adorable cakes ready to go as is. No need for frosting. They hold well if stored in an airtight tin.

baker's tip } Use two teaspoons to scoop the cream cheese mixture into the chocolate cake batter. And don't be alarmed when you see how thin the cake batter is. It's supposed to be that way.

1½ cups sifted cake flour

1 cup sugar

1 teaspoon baking soda

¼ cup unsweetened Dutch process cocoa powder

½ teaspoon salt

1 cup water

⅓ cup vegetable oil

1 tablespoon cider vinegar

1 teaspoon vanilla extract

CREAM CHEESE FILLING

8 ounces soft cream cheese

1 large egg

⅓ cup sugar

⅛ teaspoon salt

6 ounces semisweet chocolate chips

½ cup finely chopped pecans

1. **PREPARE TO BAKE.** Arrange the rack in the middle of the oven and preheat it to 400°F. Line 12 standard muffin cups with paper liners and then spritz with Baker's Joy. Place the unbroken egg in a bowl of hot tap water.

2. **MAKE THE BATTER AND FILLING.** Sift the flour, sugar, baking soda, cocoa, and salt into the bowl of a stand mixer. Add the water, oil, vinegar, and vanilla. Beat well. In a separate bowl, combine the cream cheese, egg, sugar, and salt. Stir the chocolate chips and nuts into the cream cheese mixture.

3. **BAKE THE CAKES.** Divide the cake batter among the paper-lined muffin cups, filling them one-third full. Top each with a heaping teaspoon of the cream cheese mixture. Bake until a wooden pick stuck in the edge comes out clean, 12 to 15 minutes. The middle will be liquid until it cools. Cool on a rack. Serve warm or chilled. Store in an airtight tin.

wellesley fudge cupcakes

One hundred and twenty-five years ago, the young ladies from Wellesley knew what they liked. And it's no wonder. This cake is fudgy, fast, and fabulous. Make it in a sheet pan if you wish, but we prefer cupcakes. So handy, so portable. Think of the Wellesley bakers, sticking their hand in the oven before thermostats to see how hot it was. Who knows? Maybe they baked at 400°F. All we know is that using this technique, you'll have cupcakes in 20 minutes flat. Make the frosting while the cupcakes are baking, then just dip each one into the frosting. Quick and satisfying.

baker's tip

By all means, use the microwave for melting chocolate. It's one of the microwave's finest moments. In less than a minute the chocolate will be melted. You can't actually tell by looking: It will hold its shape until you stir it with a fork or wooden skewer. Then it collapses into melted bliss.

2 large egg yolks

2 ounces (2 squares) unsweetened chocolate

½ cup water

½ cup (1 stick) soft, unsalted butter

1 cup firmly packed dark brown sugar

1 cup sifted cake flour

1 teaspoon baking powder

¼ teaspoon salt

¼ cup milk

1 teaspoon vanilla extract

1. PREPARE TO BAKE. Arrange the rack in the middle of the oven and preheat it to 400°F. Line 12 standard muffin cups with paper liners and spritz with Baker's Joy. Place 2 unbroken eggs in a bowl of hot tap water. Place the chocolate and water in a microwavable dish or in a double boiler and melt (1 to 2 minutes either way). Stir until the mixture is smooth. Set it aside.

2. MAKE THE BATTER. Cream the butter with the sugar until blended, then add the egg yolks (you won't need the whites) and melted chocolate and mix thoroughly. Sift the flour with the baking powder and salt onto a piece of wax paper. Spoon into the butter mixture in thirds, alternately with the milk and vanilla, stirring after each addition.

3. BAKE THE CAKES. Transfer the batter to the muffin cups, filling each one two-thirds full. Bake until a wooden pick comes out clean, 18 to 20 minutes. Cool on a rack.

FUDGE FROSTING

2 ounces (2 squares) unsweetened chocolate

1 tablespoon soft, unsalted butter

1 cup sifted confectioners' sugar

¼ cup milk, plus more as needed

1 teaspoon vanilla extract

4. MAKE THE FROSTING. Melt the chocolate and butter together in a microwavable bowl or double boiler until smooth. Stir in the confectioners' sugar, milk, and vanilla and blend until smooth. Let the frosting stand until the cakes are cooled, then add additional milk or cream as needed to thin the frosting. Dip each cake into the frosting.

bittersweet chocolate cupcakes MAKES 12 STANDARD CUPCAKES

Flourless but perfumed with the aroma of best-quality chocolate, these cakes melt in your mouth. Serve them the day you make them. They're fragile.

baker's tip } To grind nuts, pulse them in the food processor to a dry powder, taking care not to overprocess. You don't want to release the oil in the nuts and cause them clump up.

½ cup plus 2 tablespoons sugar, divided

2 large eggs

¾ cup whipping cream, divided

1 tablespoon unsweetened Dutch process cocoa powder

2 tablespoons unsalted butter

7 ounces best-quality bittersweet chocolate, chopped and divided

1 teaspoon vanilla extract

¼ cup ground pecans

1. **PREPARE TO BAKE.** Arrange the rack in the middle of the oven and preheat it to 400°F. Line a 12-cup muffin tin with paper liners. Spritz each paper with Baker's Joy. Sprinkle the bottom of each cup with ½ teaspoon sugar. Place the unbroken eggs in a bowl of hot tap water.

2. **MAKE THE BATTER.** Bring ½ cup of the cream, the cocoa powder, and butter to a boil in a glass measure in the microwave, about 1 minute. Stir in 5 ounces of the chopped chocolate and the vanilla. Microwave for 30 seconds, and then stir to blend.

   Beat the eggs and ½ cup sugar in a stand mixer on high speed until the batter lightens and falls away from the beaters in a wide ribbon, about 5 minutes. Gently fold in the melted chocolate mixture and the pecans. Do not overmix.

3. **BAKE THE CAKES.** Divide the batter among the paper-lined muffin cups and bake until a wooden pick comes out clean, 10 to 12 minutes. Cool on a rack.

4. **FINISH THE CAKES.** To make the ganache, heat the remaining ¼ cup cream to boiling in the microwave, then stir in the remaining chopped chocolate. Microwave for 30 seconds, and then let it stand. Whisk until smooth, then frost, using about 1 teaspoon per cake.

chocolate sweetheart
cakes with soft centers

Individual cakes with warm, soft hearts of deep, dark chocolate, these love cakes can top off a romantic dinner or stand alone as a gift to your intended.

baker's tip }
Make these cakes the day before serving if you wish, cover and refrigerate, then reheat for a few moments before turning them out onto dessert plates.

5 large eggs

¾ cup (1½ sticks) soft, unsalted butter

6 ounces best-quality bittersweet chocolate, chopped

4½ tablespoons all-purpose flour

2 tablespoons unsweetened Dutch process cocoa powder, plus more for dusting

⅓ cup sugar

1½ tablespoons Kahlúa

1 teaspoon vanilla extract

½ cup all-fruit raspberry sauce (page 124)

1 cup fresh raspberries

Confectioners' sugar, for dusting

Vanilla ice cream, for serving

1. PREPARE TO BAKE. Arrange the rack in the middle of the oven and preheat it to 400°F. Line 12 standard muffin tins (or 6 large Texas-sized ones) with paper liners and spritz them with Baker's Joy. Place the unbroken eggs in a bowl of hot tap water.

2. MAKE THE BATTER. Combine the butter and chocolate in a glass measure and melt in the microwave on high, about 2 minutes, then whisk thoroughly to yield a smooth, melted mixture. (Alternatively, stir together in a small saucepan set over low heat on the stovetop.) Sift the flour and cocoa onto a piece of wax paper. Separate the eggs and beat the egg whites in the stand mixer until foamy, then add the sugar, a spoonful at a time, and beat until the whites hold stiff, shiny peaks. Stir the liqueur, vanilla, egg yolks, and cocoa-flour mixture into the melted chocolate. Fold into the beaten egg whites just until there are no more white streaks. Don't overbeat here.

3. BAKE THE CAKES. Divide the batter among the prepared muffin cups, filling them three-fourths full. Bake just until the edges feel firm but the centers are still soft when pressed gently with your forefinger, 6 to 8 minutes. Cool for about 5 minutes on a rack before serving.

continued

4. FINISH THE CAKES. While the cakes are baking, swirl the raspberry sauce onto dessert plates and place some fresh raspberries on each plate. Invert a cake onto each dessert plate, peeling off the paper. Dust with confectioners' sugar and cocoa. Add a small scoop of vanilla ice cream.

raspberry sauce

To make raspberry sauce, simply strain fresh raspberries through a sieve or pulse in the food processor until you have a smooth pureé. Add a tiny bit of sugar, as needed, and transfer it to a ketchup dispenser. Holding the dispenser upside down, drizzle the sauce onto individual dessert plates.

5

Sheet
CAKES

Sheet cakes make terrific coffee cakes for Sunday brunch. Easy as quick breads, they're just a little sweeter. You'll note that the texture of the cakes in this category can be more fudgelike than other cakes, and the crumb can be coarser, yet they're always moist, tender, and sweet. These often serve as a traditional kid's birthday cake, for all the obvious reasons. If there was ever a time when the sizzle counts more than the steak, it's in kids' birthday cakes. What doesn't get ground up into the rug usually finds its way onto faces, hands, and birthday finery. So don't kill yourself making a cake for such an occasion. Just make a one-bowl cake that goes together quickly. Bake and serve it in a Pyrex utility pan if you don't own a shiny aluminum pan of this size. Cut the servings into little squares. It's that easy. You'll note in a number of these recipes that you don't even need to sift the flour. Just dump in the ingredients—in order—and before you can say "Jack Robinson," you've got cake. Write "I love you" or any other message you'd like on the top. Add a smiley face. Stick some candles in. Go forth!

lazy daisy sheet cake
with easy icing

How could something so simple be so sweet and pleasing? The ultimate coffee cake, this tender little thing proves you can never be too thin or too rich. Made in a 9-by-13-by-1½-inch pan, the cake is no more than ¾ inch thick, but oh so tender and lovely. And it's topped with an icing that is simply stirred together, smeared on the just-baked cake, then popped back into the oven to brown. This is the cake to choose for those mornings when you want something spectacular but don't even have the will to sift flour.

baker's tip

> What's the difference between a quick bread and this cake? Not much. Both rely on your light hand in not overmixing. The texture will be coarser than a traditional cake, but the crumb will be tender and the flavor perfumed with the goodness of vanilla and butter.

2 large eggs

½ cup milk

2 tablespoons unsalted butter

1 cup sugar

1 cup cake flour

1 teaspoon baking powder

¼ teaspoon salt

1½ teaspoons vanilla extract

EASY ICING

½ cup firmly packed dark brown sugar

¼ cup whipping cream

2 tablespoons soft, unsalted butter

1 cup sweetened, flaked coconut

½ cup chopped pecans

1. **PREPARE TO BAKE.** Arrange the rack in the middle of the oven and preheat it to 400°F. Spritz a 9-by-13-by-1½-inch shiny aluminum baking pan with Baker's Joy. Place the unbroken eggs in a bowl of hot tap water.

2. **MAKE THE BATTER.** Heat the milk and butter to boiling in a microwave, about 1 minute. Beat the eggs in a stand mixer until light, then add the sugar and beat for 1 minute. Add the flour, baking powder, and salt to the egg mixture in thirds, alternately with the milk mixture and vanilla. Beat well. (The batter will be thin.)

3. **BAKE THE CAKE.** Transfer the batter to the prepared pan and bake until a wooden pick inserted in the middle comes out clean, 15 to 20 minutes.

4. **MAKE THE ICING.** While the cake is baking, stir together the brown sugar, cream, butter, coconut, and pecans in a small bowl. Once the cake is baked, quickly pour the frosting over it and smooth it, then return the cake to the oven for a few minutes to brown the coconut. Serve warm or cool.

coco loco sheet cake

A version of this cake earned a Pillsbury Bake-Off contestant $7,500 in 1954. The method is unusual, involving cooking the egg-and-sugar mixture in a double boiler, but it yields a lovely, chewy one-layer cake in a hurry. Serve atop a fresh pineapple ring with a scoop of vanilla ice cream or a dollop of rum-scented whipped cream for the full-bore Island experience.

baker's tip

Make a great whipped cream by adding a tablespoon of sour cream to the whipping cream and sugar when you beat it. The cream will not only have a more complex flavor, but will also be more stable. You can make this whipped cream days ahead and keep it in the refrigerator.

4 large eggs

1½ cups cake flour

1 teaspoon baking powder

½ teaspoon salt

1 teaspoon instant espresso powder

1 cup firmly packed dark brown sugar

2 tablespoons unsalted butter

1 cup pecan halves

1 cup sweetened, flaked coconut

2 teaspoons vanilla extract

Vanilla ice cream or rum-scented whipped cream

Pineapple rings

1. PREPARE TO BAKE. Arrange the rack in the middle of the oven and heat it to 400°F. Spritz a 9-by-13-by-1½-inch shiny aluminum baking pan with Baker's Joy and set it aside. Place the unbroken eggs in a bowl of hot tap water.

2. MAKE THE BATTER. Combine the flour, baking powder, and salt in a large mixing bowl and fluff with a fork. Break the eggs into a glass measure. Whisk to mix, then whisk in the espresso powder, brown sugar, and butter. Microwave for 1 minute, or until the butter is melted and the mixture feels hot to the touch. (Alternatively, bring 1 inch of water to a boil in the bottom of a double boiler. Combine the egg mixture in the top of the double boiler. Place the top of the double boiler over the bottom and heat the mixture.) Dump the egg mixture into the flour and whisk. Beat with a rubber spatula until thoroughly combined. Stir in the nuts, coconut, and vanilla until thoroughly mixed.

3. BAKE THE CAKE. Transfer the batter to the prepared pan. Bake until the cake springs back at the touch when gently pressed in the center, 12 to 18 minutes. Do not overbake. Cool on a rack. Cut into squares.

4. TO SERVE, place a fresh pineapple ring on a dessert plate. Add a square of cake and top with a dollop of ice cream or whipped cream. Serve warm or at room temperature.

easy orange spice sheet cake with molten butterscotch frosting

Easy as quick bread and bursting with flavor, this makes a lovely coffee cake for a Sunday brunch or a fast after-dinner sweet. The only risk here is overbeating. Use a large bowl and a wire whisk. Just barely mix the wet and dry ingredients, then fold in the raisins and nuts. If you have a Microplane to grate the orange zest, all the better. Vanilla or rum raisin ice cream makes a great finish.

baker's tip

Correctly measured flour is one of the keys to successful cake baking, because if you pack it into the measuring cup you can actually get up to ¼ cup more flour than you intended. Open the container of flour. Take a fork and fluff the flour, then scoop gently and level it off with a straight edge. This is an easy habit to get into: fluff, scoop, and level.

2½ cups cake flour

½ teaspoon ground ginger

½ teaspoon ground cinnamon

½ teaspoon ground nutmeg

½ teaspoon ground cloves

¼ teaspoon cayenne

1½ teaspoons baking soda

½ teaspoon salt

1¼ cups firmly packed dark brown sugar

½ cup (1 stick) unsalted butter, melted

1 large egg

Grated zest and juice of 1 medium orange

¾ cup plus 2 tablespoons buttermilk

1 cup chopped walnuts

½ cup raisins

1. **PREPARE TO BAKE.** Arrange the rack in the middle of the oven and preheat it to 400°F. Spritz a 9-by-13-by-1½-inch glass or shiny aluminum baking pan with Baker's Joy.

2. **MAKE THE BATTER.** Combine the flour, ginger, cinnamon, nutmeg, cloves, cayenne, baking soda, and salt in a large bowl. Stir with a fork. In another bowl, whisk the brown sugar, melted butter, egg, orange juice, grated zest, and buttermilk. Pour the liquid into the dry ingredients, stirring just until the mixture is moistened. Fold in the nuts and raisins.

3. **BAKE THE CAKE.** Pour the batter into the prepared pan. Bake until the top springs back at the touch and a wooden pick inserted in the center comes out clean, 15 to 20 minutes. Take care not to overbake it.

FROSTING

1½ cups firmly packed dark brown sugar

5 tablespoons whipping cream

2 tablespoons unsalted butter

¼ teaspoon salt

4. FINISH THE CAKE. While the cake bakes, make the frosting. Combine, in a heavy saucepan, the brown sugar, cream, butter, and salt. Bring to a boil over medium-high heat and boil hard for 1 minute. Set it off the heat until the cake comes out of the oven. Pour the molten frosting over the hot cake. Cool on a wire rack. Cut into squares and serve. A dollop of rum raisin ice cream on top is bliss.

spicy chocolate buttermilk sheet cake

Moist, mysterious, fudgy, and spicy, this rich chocolate cake is first cousin to a brownie. Leave out the spices if you wish for an almost traditional cakelike brownie. The caramel frosting is also fudgy, so don't be surprised when your folks fight over who gets to lick the spoon.

baker's tip

Southwesterners take their kicks where they can get them, and they adore the marriage of chocolate and chiles. The optional dried ancho chile powder, available from Penzeys (see Mail-Order Sources, page 189), results in a cake with attitude. The nutmeg provides a subtle structure for the chile hit. But you'll love the tender, moist texture of this cake and may soon make it in many iterations. It's that good.

4 large eggs

4 ounces (4 squares) unsweetened chocolate

1 cup (2 sticks) soft, unsalted butter

1¾ cups sugar

2 cups cake flour

1½ teaspoons baking soda

½ teaspoon salt

½ teaspoon freshly grated nutmeg

1 teaspoon ancho chile powder (optional)

1½ cups buttermilk

1 teaspoon vanilla extract

1. PREPARE TO BAKE. Arrange the rack in the middle of the oven and preheat it to 400°F. Spritz a 9-by-13-by-1½-inch shiny aluminum baking pan with Baker's Joy. Place the unbroken eggs in a bowl of hot tap water. Melt the chocolate in the microwave in a glass measure, about 2 minutes. Stir to make a smooth paste.

2. MAKE THE BATTER. Cream the butter and sugar in a stand mixer until light. Add the eggs, one at a time, beating after each addition. Add the melted chocolate and beat well. Sift the flour, baking soda, salt, nutmeg, and chile powder, if using, onto wax paper. Add to the butter mixture in thirds, alternately with the buttermilk and vanilla.

3. BAKE THE CAKE. Turn the batter into the prepared pan and bake until a wooden pick comes out clean, 20 to 25 minutes. Cool on a rack.

CARAMEL ICING

1 cup firmly packed dark brown sugar

¼ teaspoon salt

⅓ cup whipping cream, plus more as needed

¼ cup (½ stick) soft, unsalted butter

2 cups sifted confectioners' sugar

4. FINISH THE CAKE. While the cake bakes, make the icing. Combine the brown sugar, salt, cream, and butter in a heavy saucepan with a lip and bring to a boil over medium heat, stirring. Boil hard for 2 minutes, stirring constantly, then stir in the confectioners' sugar and beat with a wooden spoon until the frosting reaches a smooth, thick, shiny consistency. Add cream as needed if it seems too thick to spread. Spread over the warm cake. Cut into squares.

chocolate sauerkraut sheet cake

This was my children's favorite birthday cake. Not only did they love the taste of this classic German cake, they also loved to get into their friends' faces after they'd just put a big bite of cake in their mouth and say, "Guess what's in this cake? Sauerkraut!" At which moment the hapless victim was sure to reply, "Yuck!" But the addition of sauerkraut assures that the cake will be moist and a good keeper.

baker's tip } You can substitute an equal portion of shredded canned beets for the sauerkraut. Just remember to rinse and thoroughly drain the beets before adding them to the batter.

3 large eggs

¾ cup (1½ sticks) soft, unsalted butter

1½ cups sugar

1 teaspoon vanilla extract

½ cup unsweetened Dutch process cocoa powder

1 teaspoon baking powder

½ teaspoon salt

1 teaspoon baking soda

2¼ cups cake flour

1 cup warm tap water

⅔ cup rinsed, chopped, and drained sauerkraut

CHOCOLATE GANACHE FROSTING

7 ounces best-quality bittersweet chocolate

1 cup whipping cream

2 tablespoons brandy or coffee liqueur, Chambord, or rum

1½ tablespoons light corn syrup

1. **PREPARE TO BAKE.** Arrange the rack in the middle of the oven and preheat it to 400°F. Spritz a 9-by-13-inch shiny aluminum baking pan with Baker's Joy. Place the unbroken eggs in a bowl of hot tap water.

2. **MAKE THE BATTER.** Cream the butter and sugar in a stand mixer until light and fluffy. Add the eggs, one at a time, and then add the vanilla. Sift the cocoa, baking powder, salt, baking soda, and flour onto a piece of wax paper. Add the flour to the creamed butter mixture in thirds, alternately with the water. Mix just until blended. Fold in the sauerkraut.

3. **BAKE THE CAKE.** Transfer the batter to the prepared pan and bake until the cake springs back at the touch and a wooden pick inserted comes out clean, 18 to 22 minutes. Cool on a rack.

4. **MAKE THE FROSTING.** Combine the chocolate and cream in a microwavable bowl or the top of a double boiler. Melt the chocolate in the microwave (1 minute) or over medium heat, and stir to mix with the cream. Add the brandy and corn syrup. Stir to make a smooth mixture. Cool to lukewarm, and then pour over the cake, tilting the cake to let the molten chocolate flow onto all surfaces.

burnt sugar sheet cake with burnt sugar icing

When my grandmother was cooking on her Kansas ranch, commercial flavorings were limited. If she wanted something other than vanilla to flavor the cake that sat on the sideboard, she had to think of something. Caramelizing sugar was well known to provide a new and welcome change. Now, in the Caribbean section of the grocery store I shop in, I see burnt sugar sold in bottles for seasoning everything from soup to callaloo.

baker's tip

To properly caramelize or "burn" sugar, you need a heavy skillet. I use my grandmother's 10-inch black cast iron skillet, still in service after almost 100 years. Dump the sugar into the skillet. Turn the burner on to medium, and stir intermittently with a wooden spoon. First you'll see the edges of the sugar begin to liquefy. Then the whole mass will begin to bubble and turn a golden brown. Be patient, keep stirring. Let every single crystal turn to syrup. Then add the boiling water and stir vigorously for a new-old favorite flavoring from the country.

BURNT SUGAR SYRUP
¾ cup sugar
¾ cup boiling water

CAKE
2 large eggs
½ cup (1 stick) soft, unsalted butter
1½ cups sugar
1 teaspoon vanilla extract
2½ cups cake flour
1 tablespoon baking powder
½ teaspoon salt
¾ cup cold water

1. MAKE THE SYRUP. Heat the sugar in a heavy skillet over medium heat, stirring constantly with a wooden spoon until the sugar dissolves and becomes dark brown. Slowly add the boiling water. Stir vigorously and set aside.

2. PREPARE TO BAKE. Arrange the rack in the middle of the oven and preheat it to 400°F. Spritz a 9-by-13-by-1½-inch shiny aluminum baking pan with Baker's Joy. Place the unbroken eggs in a bowl of hot tap water.

3. MAKE THE BATTER. Cream the butter and sugar in a stand mixer. Add the vanilla and the eggs, one at a time, beating until the mixture is fluffy and light. Sift the flour, baking powder, and salt onto a piece of wax paper. Add the flour mixture to the butter in thirds, alternately with the water, beating just to incorporate. Add 3 tablespoons of the burnt sugar syrup (reserve the rest for the frosting) and beat for 3 minutes at medium speed.

4. BAKE THE CAKE. Pour the batter into the prepared pan and bake until a wooden pick comes out clean, 20 to 25 minutes. Cool on a rack.

BURNT SUGAR FROSTING

3 ounces soft cream cheese

½ cup (1 stick) soft, unsalted butter

⅓ cup firmly packed dark brown sugar

2 cups sifted confectioners' sugar

¼ teaspoon salt

2 tablespoons burnt sugar syrup
(more as needed)

5. MAKE THE FROSTING. Beat the cream cheese and butter in a large bowl until fluffy. Add the brown sugar and beat until well blended. Add the confectioners' sugar, ½ cup at a time, beating well after each addition. Beat in the salt and 2 tablespoons of the burnt sugar syrup, adding more as needed to yield a spreading consistency. Chill until firm enough to spread, about 20 minutes. Spread onto the cooled cake.

old-fashioned jam cake

Another old-fashioned cake flavored with fruit, this cake is tender, moist, and redolent of fruit. You should choose the fruit preserves of your choice. I prefer strawberry or raspberry, but you can substitute any kind you like.

baker's tip } Always choose all-fruit preserves for the best flavor. Ordinary commercial preserves have way too much sugar to taste anything but sweet.

3 large eggs

¾ cup (1½ sticks) soft, unsalted butter

1 cup sugar

1 cup (one 10-ounce jar) your favorite all-fruit jam (try strawberry)

1½ cups cake flour

1 teaspoon baking soda

½ teaspoon ground nutmeg

½ teaspoon ground allspice

½ cup buttermilk

OLD-FASHIONED COOKED FROSTING

2 cups sugar

¼ teaspoon salt

¾ cup (1½ sticks) unsalted butter

1½ cups milk

1. **PREPARE TO BAKE.** Arrange the rack in the middle of the oven and preheat it to 400°F. Spritz a 9-by-13-by-1½-inch shiny aluminum baking pan with Baker's Joy. Place the unbroken eggs in a bowl of hot tap water.

2. **MAKE THE BATTER.** Cream the butter and sugar in a stand mixer until light. Add the eggs, one at a time, beating, and then add the jam. Combine the flour, baking soda, nutmeg, and allspice. Add to the egg mixture in thirds, alternately with the buttermilk. Beat until smooth.

3. **BAKE THE CAKE.** Pour the batter into the prepared pan and bake until a wooden pick comes out clean, 20 to 25 minutes. Cool on a rack.

4. **MAKE THE FROSTING.** While the cake bakes, combine the sugar, salt, butter, and milk in a heavy saucepan with a lip. Bring it to a boil and stir vigorously to mix. Set aside.

5. **FINISH THE CAKE.** Once the cake has cooled, pour the frosting over it, smoothing it with an offset spatula. Cut into squares.

mississippi mud sheet cake

Another winner of a cake from the Deep South, this cake rests under a layer of bumpy, melted marshmallows and a flowing river of fudge. The name cannot even begin to describe the satisfaction the cake brings to chocolate lovers. There is as much topping as bottom, as much candy as cake.

baker's tip { *Take note of this frosting. It's also great on an everyday cake or a white cake and is fast and easy to do.*

3 large eggs

½ cup (1 stick) soft, unsalted butter

1 cup sugar

¾ cup sifted cake flour

⅓ cup unsweetened Dutch process cocoa powder

1 teaspoon baking powder

½ teaspoon salt

1 teaspoon vanilla extract

1 cup chopped pecans

1 package (10½ ounces) miniature marshmallows

CHOCOLATE FROSTING

½ cup (1 stick) unsalted butter

½ cup unsweetened Dutch process cocoa powder

⅓ cup milk

¼ teaspoon salt

1 pound (1 box) confectioners' sugar

1. **PREPARE TO BAKE.** Arrange the rack in the middle of the oven and preheat it to 400°F. Spritz a 9-by-13-by-1½-inch shiny aluminum baking pan with Baker's Joy. Place the unbroken eggs in a bowl of hot tap water.

2. **MAKE THE BATTER.** Cream the butter and sugar in a stand mixer until light. Add the eggs one a time, beating. Mix the flour, cocoa, baking powder, and salt with a fork. Add to the creamed mixture, then stir in the vanilla and nuts.

3. **BAKE THE CAKE.** Spoon the batter into the prepared pan and bake until the top is barely soft to the touch, 10 to 13 minutes, then cover the top of the cake with the marshmallows. Return the cake to the oven and cook until the marshmallows are soft, about 3 minutes. Use an offset spatula to spread the hot, melting marshmallows over the cake.

4. **MAKE THE FROSTING.** Melt the butter with the cocoa in a large, heavy saucepan, and then stir in the milk, salt, and confectioners' sugar. Stir to make a smooth mixture. Once you have smoothed the marshmallows over the cake, pour the frosting over the cake and smooth it. Cool completely before cutting into squares.

fourth of july flag white sheet cake with raspberries and blueberries

MAKES ONE 9-BY-13-INCH SHEET CAKE, TO SERVE 16

Want a sheet cake you can haul to a picnic on the Fourth? What could be better than one with the stars and bars done up in raspberries and blueberries? This basic vanilla cake tastes good all by itself, but when slathered with quick buttercream and decorated with berries, it will make anyone feel patriotic—toward homemade cakes at least.

baker's tip

> If you are concerned about raw eggs, leave the yolk out of the frosting. But know that the egg yolk yields a fine, shiny, smooth texture as well as adding depth to the flavor. Raw eggs may be risky for small children, or older adults with compromised immune systems.

3 large eggs

½ cup (1 stick) soft, unsalted butter

1 cup sugar

2 teaspoons vanilla extract

2 cups sifted cake flour

2 teaspoons baking powder

½ teaspoon salt

¾ cup milk

1. PREPARE TO BAKE. Place the rack in the middle of the oven and preheat it to 400°F. Spritz a 9-by-13-by-1½-inch shiny aluminum baking pan with Baker's Joy. Place the unbroken eggs in a bowl of hot tap water.

2. MAKE THE BATTER. Beat the butter and sugar in the stand mixer until pale and fluffy, about 3 minutes. Add the eggs, one at a time, then the vanilla, and beat until thoroughly mixed, about 5 minutes. Sift the flour, baking powder, and salt onto a sheet of wax paper. Spoon in the flour in thirds, alternately with the milk. Mix just until the batter is smooth.

3. BAKE THE CAKE. Pour the batter into the prepared pan and bake until the cake begins to pull away from the sides and a wooden pick comes out clean, 18 to 20 minutes. Cool on a rack.

continued

QUICK BUTTERCREAM FROSTING

½ cup (1 stick) soft, unsalted butter

1 large egg yolk (optional)

¼ teaspoon salt

1 teaspoon vanilla or almond extract

4 cups sifted confectioners' sugar

6 tablespoons heavy cream

1 pint blueberries

1 pint raspberries

4. **MAKE THE FROSTING.** While the cake is cooling, place the butter in the mixer bowl and cream until soft, adding the egg yolk, salt, and vanilla. With the mixer on low speed, add the confectioners' sugar and cream alternately until you have a smooth mixture. Refrigerate until the cake is cool.

5. **ASSEMBLE THE CAKE.** Invert the cake onto a large serving platter. Smooth the frosting over the top and sides, using an offset spatula. Make a design on top, using the berries to create a flag. Use both raspberries and blueberries in the upper left quadrant to represent the "stars," then make the "bars" by making alternating horizontal stripes of raspberries and blueberries. Finish by alternating whole blueberries and raspberries all around the base of the cake.

6

Jelly
ROLLS

Roll 'Em Up, Roll 'Em Up, Put 'Em in the Pan

Almost as good as a bathtub full of whipped cream, cake rolls do everything. These old-fashioned cakes are quick to cook—no more than 8 to 10 minutes—and easy to manage with the new Silpat sheet or the judicious use of parchment paper. Cake rolls are glamorous to serve when cut and placed in all their coiled glory on a plate. Mostly I prefer whipped cream for a filler, but the classic version used to be made with mama's jelly and now can be made with fine European jams or good all-fruit preserves. You can pull out all the stops come the winter holiday and translate the Classic Jelly Roll into a Bûche de Noël. It may take a couple of days to get all the elements together, but your guests will be dazzled. I guarantee it.

classic jelly roll

The mother of all jelly rolls, this simple sponge cake can be rolled with nothing more than your favorite jelly, then sprinkled with confectioners' sugar, or it can become the basis for a Bûche de Noël, which I am happy to report is easier done than said.

baker's tip

The recipe is primarily a génoise, a French sponge cake that is drier than most American-style cakes. This makes it a welcome home for flavored syrups and spirits. Use your imagination to flavor the cake: Make a simple syrup and add the liqueur or flavoring of your choice. Once the cake is baked and cooled, sprinkle the flavored syrup over it in little sips before filling and rolling the cake.

5 large eggs

½ teaspoon cream of tartar

¼ teaspoon salt

½ cup sugar, divided

1 teaspoon vanilla extract

½ cup sifted cake flour

Confectioners' sugar, for dusting

¼ cup simple syrup (page 147) flavored with your favorite liqueur

FILLING
One of the following:

Pastry Cream (page 154)

Jam of your choice

Lemon Curd (page 36)

Perfect Whipped Cream (page 100)

1. PREPARE TO BAKE. Arrange the rack in the middle of the oven and preheat it to 400°F. Line a 15½-by-10½-inch shiny aluminum jelly roll pan with a Silpat or parchment paper. Place the unbroken eggs in a bowl of hot tap water for 5 minutes before separating.

2. MAKE THE BATTER. Separate the eggs into 2 large bowls. Beat the egg whites in a stand mixer on high speed with the cream of tartar and salt until soft peaks form. Add ¼ cup sugar, a spoonful at a time, and continue beating until stiff peaks form. In a second bowl, beat the egg yolks, vanilla, and remaining ¼ cup sugar until thick and ribbonlike, about 5 minutes. Fold in the flour just until blended. Gently fold the yolk mixture into the beaten whites.

3. BAKE THE CAKE. Transfer the batter to the baking pan, spreading it until you have a rectangle about 15 by 10 inches. Bake until the cake top springs back at the touch, 8 to 10 minutes. Cool on a rack for 5 minutes.

FROSTING (OPTIONAL)
One of the following:
Chocolate Ganache (page 134)
Cream Cheese Frosting (page 105)
Honest Buttercream (page 155)

4. FINISH THE CAKE. Sift confectioners' sugar onto a clean kitchen towel, then flip the warm cake onto the towel. Peel off the Silpat or paper. Starting from the long side, roll the cake and towel up together and cool completely on the rack. Unroll the cake. Sprinkle with simple syrup scented with your favorite liqueur, and then spread with pastry cream, jam, lemon curd, or perfect whipped cream. Roll up again from the long side, without the towel, and transfer to a serving plate. Dust with confectioners' sugar or frost.

simple syrup

2 cups sugar
1 cup water

Stir together the sugar and water in a medium saucepan and boil until the sugar is completely dissolved. Transfer to a jar and store in the refrigerator.

COFFEE SYRUP: Add ½ cup espresso to ¼ cup simple syrup.

CHOCOLATE SYRUP: Add 1 ounce bittersweet chocolate to ½ cup hot simple syrup and stir to melt the chocolate.

HAZELNUT SYRUP: Stir 2 tablespoons Frangelico liqueur into ¼ cup simple syrup.

YOUR FAVORITE LIQUEUR SYRUP: Stir 2 tablespoons of the liqueur of your choice into ¼ cup simple syrup.

tangerine jelly roll

Now that the Silpat is available, you can make jelly rolls in less than 30 minutes, start to finish. All you do is spread the batter onto a Silpat-covered baking pan. Meanwhile, dust a kitchen towel with confectioners' sugar, and when the cake comes out of the oven turn it out onto the cloth and roll it up to cool.

baker's tip

You'll be amazed. The new silicone-impregnated rubber mat known as the Silpat (see Mail-Order Sources, page 189) peels right off. And you have nothing to wash. Just wipe it off and wait until the next time you want cake. Roll whipped cream into the cake. It's sexy, it's easy, it's yours. Substitute flavors and aromatics at will, or try other citrus products, rose water and rose petal, peppermints crushed with a hammer and folded into the cream . . . you get the idea.

4 large eggs

¾ cup sifted cake flour

1 teaspoon baking powder

¼ teaspoon salt

⅔ cup sugar, divided

½ teaspoon vanilla extract

Confectioners' sugar, for dusting

WHIPPED CREAM FILLING

1 cup whipping cream

3 tablespoons sugar

¼ cup fresh tangerine or other citrus juice

Grated zest of 1 tangerine or other citrus

Julienned citrus zest, for garnish

1. PREPARE TO BAKE. Arrange the rack in the middle of the oven and preheat it to 400°F. Line a 15-by-10½-inch shiny aluminum jelly roll pan with a Silpat sheet or parchment paper. Spritz parchment with Baker's Joy. Place the unbroken eggs in a bowl of hot tap water.

2. MAKE THE BATTER. Sift the flour, baking powder, and salt onto a piece of wax paper. Separate the eggs. Beat the egg whites in a large bowl until soft peaks form. Gradually beat in ⅓ cup of the sugar, a tablespoon at a time, until the sugar is thoroughly dissolved and stiff peaks form. Set aside. In a large bowl, beat the egg yolks until they are thick and lemon colored, gradually adding the remaining ⅓ cup sugar and the vanilla. Sprinkle the flour mixture over the yolks and fold to mix. Fold gently into the egg white mixture.

3. BAKE THE CAKE. Spread the batter on the prepared pan and bake until the top springs back when touched, 8 to 12 minutes. Meanwhile, dust a kitchen towel with confectioners' sugar. When the cake is baked, turn it out onto the towel and peel the Silpat or parchment off. Starting from the long side, carefully roll up the warm cake with the cloth and set it aside to cool.

4. FILL THE CAKE. Whip the cream with the sugar and citrus juice until stiff peaks form. Fold in the grated zest. Unroll the cake and spread the whipped cream inside. Reroll and place on a serving plate. Dust the top with additional confectioners' sugar, and garnish with julienned citrus zest.

sweet potato cake roll

Thanksgiving offers a fine opportunity for an autumnal roll that is less sweet than pumpkin pie and more complex than its simple construction would reveal.

baker's tip { For best results, microwave a sweet potato you have jabbed with a fork, then scrape out and mash the purée with a fork. Alternatively, use pumpkin purée from a can, or place a small sugar pumpkin in the microwave after you've jabbed it with a knife and cook until soft, about 10 minutes. Scrape out and discard the seeds, then scrape out and mash the flesh.

½ cup chopped hazelnuts

3 large eggs

1 cup sugar

⅔ cup cooked sweet potato or pumpkin purée

1 tablepoon fresh lemon juice

Grated zest of ½ lemon

¾ cup sifted cake flour

1 teaspoon baking powder

2 teaspoons ground cinnamon

1 teaspoon ground ginger

½ teaspoon ground nutmeg

½ teaspoon salt

Confectioners' sugar, for dusting

CREAM CHEESE FILLING

6 ounces soft cream cheese

½ cup (1 stick) soft, unsalted butter

1 cup sifted confectioners' sugar, plus more for sprinkling

1 teaspoon vanilla extract

TOPPING (OPTIONAL)

Whipped cream

Chopped hazelnuts

1. PREPARE TO BAKE. Arrange the rack in the middle of the oven and preheat it to 400°F. Line a 15½-by-10-inch shiny aluminum jelly roll pan with a Silpat or parchment paper. Spritz with Baker's Joy. Line the pan with the chopped nuts. Place the unbroken eggs in a bowl of hot tap water for about 5 minutes.

2. MAKE THE CAKE. Beat the eggs in a stand mixer for 5 minutes, adding the sugar, a spoonful at a time. Fold in the sweet potato, lemon juice, and zest. Sift the flour, baking powder, cinnamon, ginger, nutmeg, and salt onto a piece of wax paper and fold into the pumpkin mixture.

3. BAKE THE CAKE. Transfer the batter to the baking pan and bake until the top springs back at the touch, 8 to 10 minutes. Cool on a rack for 5 minutes.

4. FINISH THE CAKE. Dust a clean kitchen towel with confectioners' sugar. Flip the cake onto the towel and carefully peel away the Silpat or parchment. Starting at the long side, roll the cake and towel together, then cool completely on the rack. For the filling, whip the cream cheese and butter until light, then add the confectioners' sugar and vanilla and beat until smooth and spreadable. Unroll the cool cake and spread with the filling. Reroll and transfer to a serving plate. Sprinkle with confectioners' sugar or top with whipped cream and additional chopped hazelnuts.

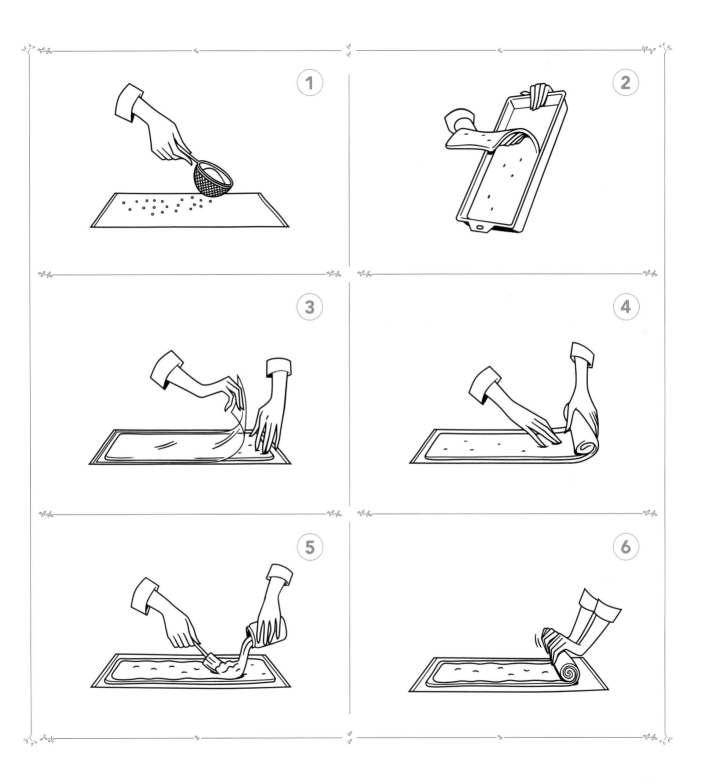

bûche de noël

The French make a traditional cake shaped like a Yule log called the Bûche de Noël, which means "Christmas log." The cake is served at the grand feast of the season, *le Reveillon,* which takes place after midnight mass on Christmas Eve. The menu for the meal varies according to regional culinary tradition, but it concludes with the Bûche de Noël. Although the process of making this dessert takes two days, what the heck. It's Christmas.

baker's tip

> The classic Christmas roll made famous in France is a simple assemblage of three elements: cake, filling, and frosting. I like to serve this roll on a slab of marble and decorate it with ribbon candy (see Mail-Order Sources, page 189) and meringue mushrooms.

ONE DAY BEFORE YOU ARE PLANNING TO SERVE, MAKE THE FOLLOWING:

A jelly roll cake using the recipe for Classic Jelly Roll (page 146) or the Chocolate Cake Roll (page 160). Roll it in a towel and cover the towel with a loose coating of plastic wrap. Set aside.

Pastry Cream (page 154). Refrigerate.

Simple Syrup (page 147).

Honest Buttercream (page 155). Cover and refrigerate.

Confectioners' sugar, for dusting

Unsweetened cocoa powder, for dusting

Meringue Mushrooms (page 156).

ON THE DAY YOU ARE PLANNING TO SERVE, DO THE FOLLOWING:

1. Carefully unroll the cake.

2. Bring the pastry cream and buttercream to room temperature. Do not use the microwave. Allow 1 hour on the countertop for each one.

3. Sprinkle the cake generously with flavored simple syrup.

4. Spread the cake with 1 cup pastry cream, then carefully reroll it and place it on the marble. With each roll, brush additional syrup on the roll. Saw off both ends at an angle.

5. Frost the cake with the buttercream. Use a fork to swirl the buttercream into "tree trunk" lines, adding a knot or two by swirling the fork. Sprinkle the frosting with a bit of unsweetened cocoa powder and confectioners' sugar. Decorate with meringue mushrooms, ribbon candy, or whatever Christmas décor strikes your fancy.

6. Refrigerate until serving time. Cut into thin slices to serve.

pastry cream

In addition to filling cakes with pastry cream, you can use it to make a Boston cream pie (page 83) or simply serve it with fruit or berries for its own lovely dessert. Made in the microwave, it is foolproof. Just remember to allow it time to chill before serving. You can make this up to a week in advance, if you keep it covered in the refrigerator. It makes a fine filling for the Bûche de Noël. Stud it with fruits or nuts if you wish.

2 cups whole milk

4 large egg yolks

¼ teaspoon salt

½ cup sugar

1 tablespoon golden rum, such as Bacardi Ocho, or vanilla extract

2 teaspoons vanilla extract

¼ cup cornstarch

¼ cup (½ stick) unsalted butter, cut into pieces

Heat the milk in a glass quart measure or bowl in the microwave for 4 minutes. Meanwhile, beat the egg yolks and salt in a stand mixer until thick, about 3 minutes, then add the sugar, a spoonful at a time, beating until the mixture is pale and thick. Toss in the rum, vanilla, and cornstarch and beat until smooth. Drizzle in a little of the hot milk, and then add all the egg mixture to the milk and whisk thoroughly. Heat in the microwave for 2 minutes, then whisk thoroughly and heat again until thick, 2 or 3 more minutes. Whisk in the butter, a piece at a time, and keep whisking until the mixture is smooth. Cover and refrigerate until ready to use.

honest buttercream

Frost everything from layer cakes to cupcakes to a Bûche de Noël with this buttercream. Make it as much as a week ahead and keep it, covered, in the refrigerator, or freeze it for up to a month. Bring it to room temperature on the countertop (never in the microwave) and beat with a stand mixer before spreading. Use the leftover egg yolks to make pastry cream.

baker's tip }

This recipe uses raw egg whites. If you are concerned about this, or have little children or elderly people in your household, reconstitute dried egg whites, such as Wilton or "Just Whites," and go forth.

4 large eggs
⅔ cup water
1½ cups sugar, divided
¼ teaspoon salt
2 cups (4 sticks) soft, unsalted butter
2 teaspoons vanilla extract

1. PREPARE TO MAKE THE BUTTERCREAM. Place the eggs in a bowl of hot tap water. Get out a candy thermometer and a heavy saucepan with a lip (like Le Creuset).

2. MAKE THE BUTTERCREAM. Stir the water and 1⅓ cups of the sugar in the pan until the sugar dissolves, and then bring to a boil, covered. When the syrup reaches a boil, place the candy thermometer in the pan and cook until the syrup reaches 238°F. Meanwhile, separate the eggs and beat the whites with the salt in a stand mixer until foamy, then add the remaining sugar and beat to soft peaks. Once the syrup is 238°F, remove it from the heat and, with the mixer running, pour it in a thin stream into the beaten egg whites. Continue beating until the mixture is cool to the touch, at least 5 minutes and up to 15. (Stick your finger into it to check. Okay. Go ahead. Lick your finger.) Now, with the mixer at medium speed, begin pinching off pieces of butter and tossing them in, beating all the while. Add the vanilla and continue beating until the buttercream looks smooth. Use it immediately, or cover and refrigerate or freeze until needed.

meringue mushrooms

Maida Heatter, famed pastry chef of the sixties, brought meringue mushrooms into the kitchens of American home cooks. They are a real craft and may take a while to perfect, but if you've ever tramped through the woods, you've seen a bunch of misshapen ones in nature too, so don't fret if yours don't look picture perfect.

baker's tip } Remember to warm the unbroken eggs in a bowl of hot tap water before separating them, and don't let one speck of egg yolk get into the egg whites before you beat them into submission.

2 large egg whites

¼ teaspoon cream of tartar

½ cup sugar

2 tablespoons bittersweet chocolate chips

Unsweetened cocoa powder for dusting

1. **MAKE THE MERINGUE.** Warm 2 unbroken eggs in a bowl of hot tap water for about 5 minutes, then separate carefully. Beat the egg whites until frothy. (You won't need the yolks.) Add the cream of tartar and increase the mixer speed, then beat until soft peaks form. Start adding the sugar, a spoonful at a time. Beat until stiff, glossy peaks form, about 5 minutes.

2. **FORM THE MUSHROOMS.** Place the meringue in a large resealable plastic bag or pastry bag and push the mixture toward one corner, folding the other corner over and then twisting, allowing you to control the meringue. Cut off just the very tip of the exposed corner so the meringue can exit the bag. Then try it out by dotting 4 small beads of meringue at the corners of a baking sheet. Set a sheet of parchment paper over the top; the meringue beads will act as glue.

Make the mushroom caps by holding the bag over the parchment paper and pushing until a 1-inch mound of meringue forms. Wet the tip of your finger with water and gently round off any peaks to make a smooth surface.

For the mushroom stems, form peaks on smaller mounds of meringue by pulling the bag up and away from the surface as you push.

3. **BAKE THE MUSHROOMS.** Place the baking sheet in a 200°F oven for 2 hours. Then turn off the heat and leave the meringue in the oven to dry for 1 hour or overnight.

4. **CONSTRUCT THE MUSHROOMS.** Melt the chocolate chips in the microwave for about 30 seconds, or until melted. Stir with a skewer. Make a hole smaller than a pea in the bottom of a mushroom cap with a toothpick or skewer. Dip the tip of a stem in the melted chocolate and press it into the hole in the cap. Allow the chocolate "glue" to harden (it only takes a minute). Place the mushroom upright on its stem, and dust the cap lightly with cocoa powder. To use on a bûche de Noël, add chocolate "glue" to the top of the cake roll and fix the meringue mushrooms to the cake in an artful pattern.

polenta lemon roll-up with strawberries and whipped cream

The addition of polenta or cornmeal adds a crunchy texture to this cake roll and, if you choose yellow cornmeal, a lovely golden hue. The liberal use of fresh lemon juice and zest gives a puckery sweetness to the filling that's like a lemon meringue pie, only better.

baker's tip

> This is a big cake roll and requires a long serving plate, at least 15 inches long. Allow plenty of room for both the filling and the fruit so the resulting cake will look as abundant on the plate as it actually is.

3 large eggs

1 pint strawberries, divided

1 cup plus 2 tablespoons sugar, divided

½ teaspoon finely milled black pepper

½ cup fresh lemon juice

Grated zest of ½ lemon

1 teaspoon vanilla extract

½ cup sifted cake flour

½ cup yellow cornmeal or polenta

1 teaspoon baking powder

½ teaspoon salt

Confectioners' sugar, for dusting

1. **PREPARE TO BAKE.** Arrange the rack in the middle of the oven and preheat it to 400°F. Line a 15½-by-10-inch shiny aluminum jelly roll pan with a Silpat or parchment paper. Place the unbroken eggs in a bowl of hot tap water. Chop ½ cup of the strawberries, and hull the remaining berries. Sprinkle the berries with 2 tablespoons of the sugar and the pepper, and then refrigerate, covered.

2. **MAKE THE BATTER.** Beat the eggs until thick, about 5 minutes, adding the remaining 1 cup sugar by the spoonful. Add the lemon juice, zest, and vanilla. Sift the flour, cornmeal, baking powder, and salt onto a piece of wax paper, and then spoon into the egg mixture, beating just until combined. Don't overbeat.

3. **BAKE THE CAKE.** Pour the batter into the pan and bake until the top springs back at the touch, 8 to 10 minutes. Cool on a rack for 5 minutes.
    Dust a kitchen towel with confectioners' sugar, then flip the cake onto the towel and carefully peel off the Silpat or paper. Starting from the long side, roll the cake and towel together and cool on the rack.

continued

CLEAR LEMON JELLY FILLING

¾ cup sugar

3 tablespoons cornstarch

½ teaspoon salt

¾ cup water

⅓ cup fresh lemon juice

Grated zest of ½ lemon

1 tablespoon butter

Perfect Whipped Cream (page 100)

Curls of lemon zest, for garnish

4. MAKE THE FILLING. Mix the sugar, cornstarch, and salt in a heavy saucepan with a lip, such as Le Creuset. Stir in the water and lemon juice and cook, stirring, until the mixture thickens and boils. Boil and stir for 1 minute, then remove from the heat and stir in the lemon zest and butter. Place a piece of wax paper onto the surface, and then refrigerate until it's time to fill the cake.

5. FINISH THE CAKE. Unroll the cake, and spread it with the filling. Sprinkle with the chopped strawberries. Reroll without the towel and transfer to a serving plate. Refrigerate until serving time. Top with perfect whipped cream. Finish with curls of lemon zest and whole strawberries. Cut into thick slices.

double whammy chocolate cake roll with raspberries

MAKES 1 CAKE ROLL,
TO SERVE 10 TO 12 PEOPLE

You will adore this cake, basically a chocolate sponge cake, with raspberries both rolled up into the middle and decorating the plate as in this recipe. It also makes an ideal base for a Bûche de Noël. The cake has a well-developed chocolate flavor, is sturdy as a kitchen sponge, and holds both filling and frosting admirably. When combined with the filling given here or a pastry cream (page 154) filling for less chocolate punch and buttercream frosting (page 155), and then trimmed with your own home-made meringue mushrooms (page 156), this cake will make a spectacular finish to a holiday dinner.

baker's tip
> You can roll the cake in a kitchen towel dusted with confectioners' sugar or in plain wax or parchment paper coated with the sugar. Just be sure to allow enough time for the cake, the filling, and the frosting to cool before assembling the cake.

4 large eggs

⅔ cup sugar, divided

½ teaspoon vanilla or other extract

⅔ cup all-purpose unbleached flour

3 tablespoons unsweetened Dutch process cocoa powder

1 teaspoon baking powder

¼ teaspoon salt

Confectioners' sugar, for dusting

1. PREPARE TO BAKE. Arrange the rack in the middle of the oven and preheat it to 400° F. Line one 11-by-17-inch shiny aluminum jelly roll pan with a Silpat or parchment. If using parchment, spritz it with Baker's Joy. Place the unbroken eggs in a bowl of hot tap water for 5 minutes before separating.

2. MAKE THE BATTER. Separate the eggs. Beat the egg whites in a large bowl until soft peaks form. Gradually beat in ⅓ cup of the sugar, a tablespoon at a time, until the sugar is thoroughly dissolved and stiff peaks form. Set aside. In a large bowl, without washing the beaters, beat the egg yolks until they are thick and lemon colored, gradually adding the remaining ⅓ cup sugar and vanilla. Sift the flour, cocoa, baking powder, and salt onto a piece of wax paper. Sprinkle the flour mixture over the yolks and fold to mix. Fold gently into the egg white mixture.

3. BAKE THE CAKE. Spread the batter on the prepared pan and bake until the top springs back when touched, 8 to 12 minutes. Cool on a rack for 5 minutes. Meanwhile, dust a kitchen towel or a sheet of parchment paper with confectioners' sugar. Turn the cake out onto the paper and peel the Silpat off. Starting from the long side, carefully roll the warm cake with the cloth or paper and set aside to cool.

CHOCOLATE CREAM CHEESE FILLING

1 cup whipping cream

1 cup sifted confectioners'
sugar, divided

2 ounces (2 squares) unsweetened
chocolate

8 ounces cream cheese

1 pint fresh raspberries

Confectioners' sugar, for dusting

1 teaspoon unsweetened Dutch
process cocoa powder

Semisweet chocolate curls (see note)

4. FINISH THE CAKE. To make the filling, whip the cream with ½ cup of the confectioners' sugar until stiff peaks form. Place the unsweetened chocolate in a glass bowl and microwave on high for 2 minutes, or until almost melted, stirring after 1 minute. Let cool. Place the cream cheese in a medium bowl and beat with a mixer until smooth. Gradually add the melted chocolate and remaining ½ cup confectioners' sugar. The mixture will be thick. Finally, gently fold in the whipped cream. Open the cake and spread the chocolate filling inside, leaving a ½-inch border. Add a few raspberries if you wish. Reroll and place on a serving plate, seam side down. Dust the top with additional confectioners' sugar and cocoa, then garnish with chocolate curls and additional raspberries. Chill until serving time. Cut into thick slices.

note: To make chocolate curls, simply use a potato peeler to shave off curls from a semisweet chocolate bar.

7

Just
LOAFING

Rich, butter-drenched loaf cakes are popular because they keep well, often require no frosting, and deliver in the flavor department. Traditional loaf cakes bake for up to 1 hour and 15 minutes, but using this new method, they will be done in 35 to 45 minutes, knocking about half an hour off the cooking time. Long known as easy to put together, they bake at the higher temperature quite nicely, with a couple of caveats. Because you are working with a large volume of batter in a brick shape, it is imperative that the center be given the best chance to cook through before the top browns. Once you've poured the batter into the prepared pan, lay a sheet of aluminum foil you've spritzed with Baker's Joy—loosely and shiny side down—over the top of the pan. Bake for 25 minutes, then remove the foil and bake for about 20 minutes more, or until the loaf is baked through.

Perhaps more than with any other shape cake, it is critical that you not let a bunch of cold air blast into the oven and cause the cake to fall. Whisk the foil off quickly, and carefully close the oven door. After 20 more minutes of baking, open the oven and examine the loaf. Is it golden brown? Does the top mound up slightly? Is it beginning to pull away from the pan? If you press the center with your forefinger, does it bounce back? Poke a wooden pick in the middle. Does it come out clean?

When you can answer yes to these questions, remove the loaf and let it cool in the pan on a rack for 5 minutes, then flip it out to cool completely. Notice the gorgeous crisp crust. Cut into the cooled cake and take a look at the even, aromatic crumb. Wrap these cakes tightly in foil or plastic wrap and they will keep for days.

applesauce date loaf cake

Great for camping trips, this loaf can be made at home, wrapped in foil, and carried along. The aroma of cloves is powerful, and the applesauce means it stays moist for days. Unless the bears get it while you snooze.

baker's tip 〉 For ease of preparation, buy pitted, chopped dates.

2 large eggs

¼ cup golden rum, such as Bacardi Ocho

½ cup pitted, chopped dates

¼ cup (½ stick) soft, unsalted butter

½ cup granulated sugar

¼ cup firmly packed dark brown sugar

1 cup sifted cake flour

1 teaspoon ground cinnamon

½ teaspoon ground cloves

½ teaspoon baking soda

½ teaspoon freshly grated nutmeg

½ teaspoon salt

¾ cup applesauce

½ cup chopped walnuts

½ cup honey

3 tablespoons unsalted butter

1. **PREPARE TO BAKE.** Arrange the rack in the middle of the oven and preheat it to 400°F. Spritz a 9-by-5-inch shiny aluminum loaf pan and the shiny side of a piece of foil large enough to cover the top of the pan with Baker's Joy. Place the unbroken eggs in a bowl of hot tap water. Heat the rum and dates in a micro-wavable dish in the microwave (or on the stovetop in a pan) just until it comes to a boil, about 1 minute. Cool. Strain, reserving both the dates and the liquid.

2. **MAKE THE BATTER.** Cream the soft butter with the sugars until light and fluffy, about 3 minutes. Add the eggs, one at time, beating continuously. Sift the flour, cinnamon, cloves, baking soda, nutmeg, and salt onto a piece of wax paper. Add the applesauce to the creamed mixture in thirds, alternately with the flour mix-ture, beating just until the batter is combined. Fold in the dates and walnuts.

3. **BAKE THE CAKE.** Pour the batter into the prepared pan, lay the foil, shiny side down, lightly over the top, and bake for 25 minutes. Quickly whisk away the foil and continue to bake until a wooden pick comes out clean, about 20 minutes more. Cool in the pan on a rack for 5 minutes, then flip the cake out onto the rack and cool completely.

4. **FINISH THE CAKE.** Make a glaze by combining the rum reserved from soaking the dates with the honey and butter in a small, heavy saucepan. Bring to a boil. Drizzle over the warm cake.

apricot walnut loaf cake

Almost pure white, studded with glorious apricots and nuts, this lovely tea cake calls for nothing more than a sprinkling of confectioners' sugar.

baker's tip

Chop the apricots and nuts on a board with a sharp chef's knife, or toss them with a little flour and pulse in the food processor just until you have small bits of fruit or nuts. Take care not to overprocess. No more than four or five pulses should do the job.

1 large egg

8 ounces dried apricots, chopped

1 cup water

½ cup (1 stick) soft, unsalted butter

½ cup sugar

2 cups sifted cake flour

1 teaspoon baking powder

½ teaspoon salt

⅓ cup orange juice

½ cup walnut pieces

1. PREPARE TO BAKE. Arrange the rack in the middle of the oven and preheat it to 400°F. Spritz a 9-by-5-inch shiny aluminum loaf pan and the shiny side of a piece of aluminum foil large enough to cover the top of the pan with Baker's Joy. Place the unbroken egg in a bowl of hot tap water. Heat the apricots and water in a small saucepan until the fruit is plumped. Set aside to cool.

2. MAKE THE BATTER. Cream the butter until light, then add the sugar and beat until fluffy. Add the egg and beat well. Add the flour, baking powder, and salt in thirds, alternately with the orange juice and ¼ cup of the apricot soaking liquid. Mix just until moistened. Fold in the drained apricots and nuts.

3. BAKE THE CAKE. Pour the batter into the prepared pan, lay the foil, shiny side down, loosely over the top, and bake for 25 minutes. Quickly remove the foil and continue to bake until a wooden pick inserted in the middle comes out clean, about 20 more minutes. Cool in the pan on a rack for 5 minutes, then flip it out onto the rack to cool completely. Wrap in plastic wrap to store.

brown sugar loaf cake

Luscious and sweet, this dark, caramel-colored sugar cake is crumbly, spicy, and everything nice.

baker's tip

If you'd like to kick up the spice a notch, choose cinnamon sticks and grate them yourself using a Microplane (see Mail-Order Sources, page 189). Grind your own cloves in a spice grinder. The resulting uptick in taste will make the extra effort worth it.

2 large eggs, divided

¼ cup (½ stick) soft, unsalted butter

1 cup firmly packed dark brown sugar

1¼ cups sifted cake flour, divided

½ cup pecan halves

1½ teaspoons baking powder

½ teaspoon salt

1 teaspoon ground cinnamon

½ teaspoon ground cloves

½ cup milk

1 teaspoon vanilla extract

1. **PREPARE TO BAKE.** Arrange the rack in the middle of the oven and preheat it to 400°F. Spritz a 9-by-5-inch shiny aluminum loaf pan and the shiny side of a piece of aluminum foil large enough to cover the top of the pan with Baker's Joy. Place the unbroken eggs in a bowl of hot tap water.

2. **MAKE THE BATTER.** Cream the butter until light, then add the brown sugar and beat until fluffy. Separate the eggs. Add 2 of the egg yolks, one at a time, beating well after each addition, then add 1 egg white and beat well (you won't need the remaining egg whites). Toss ¼ cup of the flour with the nuts. Mix the remaining 1 cup flour with the baking powder, salt, cinnamon, and cloves, then add to the butter mixture in thirds, alternately with the milk and vanilla. Fold in the nuts.

3. **BAKE THE CAKE.** Pour the batter into the prepared pan, lay the foil, shiny side down, loosely over the top, and bake for 25 minutes. Quickly remove the foil and continue baking until a wooden pick inserted in the middle comes out clean, about 20 more minutes. Cool in the pan on a rack for 5 minutes, then turn out onto the rack to cool completely. Store wrapped tightly in plastic.

chocolate chocolate chip loaf cake

Doubly dense with Dutch process cocoa and chocolate chips, this cake is best served in thin slices, with just a dollop of whipped cream.

baker's tip

Buy the best-quality bittersweet chips you can find, for best results. Check the label carefully to be sure you're not getting artificial chocolate. If you want the pluperfect best, don't buy chocolate chips at all, but a best-quality 7-ounce bar that you chop and fold into the cake.

2 large eggs

¾ cup sugar

2 teaspoons vanilla extract

10 tablespoons (1¼ sticks) soft, unsalted butter

1 cup buttermilk

1¾ cups sifted cake flour

¼ cup unsweetened Dutch process cocoa powder

1 teaspoon baking powder

½ teaspoon baking soda

¾ cup (7 ounces) bittersweet chocolate chips

1. **PREPARE TO BAKE.** Arrange the rack in the middle of the oven and preheat it to 400°F. Spritz a 9-by-5-inch shiny aluminum loaf pan and the shiny side of a piece of aluminum foil large enough to cover the top of the pan with Baker's Joy. Place the unbroken eggs in a bowl of hot tap water for about 5 minutes.

2. **MAKE THE BATTER.** Beat the sugar, eggs, and vanilla in a stand mixer until thick and blended. Add the butter and buttermilk and beat well. Sift the flour, cocoa, baking powder, and baking soda onto a piece of wax paper, then add to the batter and stir just until well blended. Stir in the chocolate chips.

3. **BAKE THE CAKE.** Pour the batter into the prepared pan, lay the shiny side of the foil loosely over it, and bake for 25 minutes. Quickly whisk off the foil and continue to bake until a wooden pick comes out clean, about 20 more minutes. Cool in the pan on a rack for 5 minutes, then turn the cake out onto the rack to cool completely. Store wrapped in plastic.

cranberry orange nut loaf
with streusel topping

Whip it up in one bowl, using nothing but a fork, throw it in the oven, and then before you know it, you'll have a steaming hot, aromatic tea cake just made for Sunday brunch or rainy afternoons.

baker's tip

> It's hard to say whether this is a cake or a sweet bread, but the method is more quick bread than cake. The main caveat is not to overdo it. Barely mix the wet ingredients into the dry before transferring the mixture to a loaf pan for baking. You'll be rewarded with a tender crumb that flakes in your hand and a cake that's moist, sweet, and aromatic with cranberries and nuts.

1 large egg

1¼ cups sifted cake flour

¾ cup sugar

½ cup sweetened dried cranberries

½ cup walnut pieces

1½ teaspoons baking powder

½ teaspoon salt

¾ cup sour cream

¼ cup water

2 tablespoons unsalted butter, melted

2 tablespoons grated orange zest

1. PREPARE TO BAKE. Arrange the rack in the middle of the oven and preheat it to 400°F. Spritz a 9-by-5-inch shiny aluminum loaf pan and the shiny side of a piece of aluminum foil large enough to cover the top of the pan with Baker's Joy. Place the unbroken egg in a bowl of hot tap water.

2. MAKE THE BATTER. Add the flour to a large mixing bowl with the sugar, cranberries, walnuts, baking powder, and salt. Toss to mix. Remove and hold aside 2 tablespoons of the flour mixture. Make a well in the center. Combine the sour cream, water, melted butter, orange zest, and egg in a glass measure. Whisk with a fork, then pour into the flour mixture. Stir until well mixed.

3. BAKE THE CAKE. Transfer the batter to the loaf pan. Top with the reserved flour-sugar mixture for a streusel topping. Lay the shiny side of the foil down loosely over the top and bake for 25 minutes. Quickly whisk off the foil and bake for 10 to 20 more minutes, or until a wooden pick comes out clean. Cool in the pan on a rack for 5 minutes, then turn it out onto the rack to cool. Cut into slices while warm. Best served the day it's made.

lemon loaf cake soaked
with lemon syrup

Here is a great cake to give away during the holidays. Bake it in two mini-loaf pans if you wish. Just knock 15 minutes off the baking time. Wrap them in cellophane, tie on a bow, and it's Merry Christmas time.

baker's tip

The latest science says that the antioxidant properties in citrus are located in the rind, not in the juice, so just think of these cakes as your nod to health and long life.

2 large eggs

½ cup (1 stick) soft, unsalted butter

1¼ cups sugar, divided

¼ cup grated lemon zest (from 3 lemons)

1½ cups sifted cake flour

½ teaspoon baking powder

½ teaspoon baking soda

½ teaspoon salt

½ cup fresh lemon juice, divided

⅓ cup buttermilk

1 teaspoon vanilla extract

GLAZE

1 cup sifted confectioners' sugar

2 tablespoons fresh lemon juice

1. **PREPARE TO BAKE.** Arrange the rack in the middle of the oven and preheat it to 400°F. Spritz one 9-by-5-inch shiny aluminum loaf pan (or 2 mini-loaf pans) and the shiny side of a piece of aluminum foil large enough to cover the top of the pan with Baker's Joy. Place the unbroken eggs in a bowl of hot tap water.

2. **MAKE THE BATTER.** Cream the butter and 1 cup of the sugar in a stand mixer until light and fluffy. Add the eggs, one at a time, and continue beating. Add the lemon zest. Sift the flour, baking powder, baking soda, and salt onto a sheet of wax paper. Combine 2 tablespoons of the lemon juice with the buttermilk and vanilla in a glass measure. Add the flour to the creamed mixture in thirds, alternately with the buttermilk.

3. **BAKE THE CAKE.** Pour the batter into the prepared pan. Lay the shiny side of the foil loosely over the top. Bake for 25 minutes, then quickly remove the foil and continue to bake for 10 to 15 minutes more, or until a wooden pick comes out clean.

4. **MAKE THE SYRUP.** While the cake bakes, combine the remaining ¼ cup sugar and 6 tablespoons lemon juice in a small saucepan and cook over low heat until the sugar dissolves.

5. **FINISH THE CAKE.** Cool the cake in the pan on a rack for 5 minutes, then flip out onto the rack set over a large tray. Spoon the lemon syrup over the cake and cool completely. Stir the confectioners' sugar and lemon juice together for the glaze and drizzle over the cooled cake.

super cider fruit and nut loaf

Autumn on a plate, this hearty cake is rich with the aroma of apple cider. To our palate, it's best when made with dried apples and cranberries. Throw in a handful of crystallized ginger to zip it up to another level.

baker's tip } To quickly chop the fruits, toss them with a tablespoon of flour so the pieces don't stick together, then pulse them in a food processor, just until chopped.

2 large eggs

1½ cups fresh apple cider or hard cider, divided

¾ cup dried fruits of your choice (raisins, cherries, currants, cranberries, apples, pears, apricots, or crystallized ginger), chopped

½ cup (1 stick) soft, unsalted butter

½ cup firmly packed dark brown sugar

1¼ cups plus 1 tablespoon sifted cake flour, divided

1 teaspoon ground ginger

½ teaspoon ground nutmeg

½ teaspoon baking soda

½ cup chopped walnuts

1. **PREPARE TO BAKE.** Arrange the rack in the middle of the oven and preheat it to 400°F. Spritz one 9-by-5-inch shiny aluminum loaf pan and the shiny side of a piece of aluminum foil large enough to cover the top of the pan with Baker's Joy. Place the unbroken eggs in a bowl of hot tap water. Heat ½ cup of the cider to a simmer in a small saucepan, then add the fruit and set aside for 10 minutes while you complete the batter. Drain in a colander.

2. **MAKE THE BATTER.** Cream the butter and brown sugar together in a stand mixer. Sift 1¼ cups of the flour, the ginger, nutmeg, and baking soda together onto a sheet of wax paper. Break the eggs into the creamed mixture, one at a time, and continue beating. Add the flour mixture to the creamed mixture in thirds, alternately with the remaining 1 cup of cider, making a smooth batter. Combine the walnuts and fruit in a small bowl and sprinkle with the remaining 1 tablespoon flour. Toss to coat, and then fold into the batter.

3. **BAKE THE CAKE.** Pour the batter into the loaf pan, cover loosely with the foil, shiny side down, and bake for 25 minutes. Quickly whisk off the foil and continue to bake until a wooden pick comes out clean, about 20 more minutes. Cool in the pan on a rack for 5 minutes, then turn the cake out, cool completely, and wrap tightly in foil or plastic wrap. Keeps for at least 1 week.

pineapple macadamia nut loaf

A certain famous mail-order food company made its reputation for cakes by selling a version of this cake. And why not? It's not too sweet, and it's luscious with the perfume of pineapple and rich with the crunch of macadamia nuts. No doubt invented in Hawaii, this is one regional favorite we're all happy to love as one of our own. It keeps exceptionally well because of the moist pineapple in it.

baker's tip

Because of their golf ball shape, macadamias can be a bear to chop. I usually smash them with the side of the chef's knife, to knock them into submission before I attempt to finely chop them. Alternatively, you could pulse them in a food processor, taking care not to overprocess them. Just four or five pulses will do it.

4 pineapple rings

4 maraschino cherries (optional)

2 tablespoons dark brown sugar

2 large eggs

½ cup granulated sugar

¼ cup vegetable oil

⅓ cup pineapple juice

¼ cup canned, crushed pineapple with juice

1 teaspoon vanilla extract

1½ teaspoons baking powder

1½ cups sifted cake flour

½ cup chopped macadamia nuts

1. **PREPARE TO BAKE.** Arrange the rack in the middle of the oven and preheat it to 400°F. Spritz a 9-by-5-inch shiny aluminum loaf pan and the shiny side of a piece of aluminum foil large enough to cover the top of the pan with Baker's Joy. Arrange the drained pineapple rings in the bottom of the pan. Put a cherry in the middle of each one, and then sprinkle with the brown sugar. Place the unbroken eggs in a bowl of hot tap water for about 5 minutes.

2. **MAKE THE BATTER.** Combine the eggs, sugar, oil, juice, pineapple, and vanilla in a large bowl and whisk thoroughly. Sift the baking powder and flour onto a piece of wax paper, then spoon into the liquid. Whisk thoroughly, and then fold in the nuts.

3. **BAKE THE CAKE.** Pour the batter into the prepared pan, lay the piece of foil loosely over the top, shiny side down, and bake for 25 minutes. Quickly remove the foil and continue to bake until a wooden pick comes out clean, about 20 more minutes. Cool in the pan on a rack for 10 minutes, then flip it out onto the rack to finish cooling. Store wrapped in plastic.

prune-raisin loaf cake

Heady with the aroma of prunes, this dark, spicy loaf will keep for at least 2 weeks if you wrap it tightly in plastic wrap.

baker's tip
> For added flavor notes, buy lemon- or orange-flavored prunes. For a complete change of pace, substitute dried figs for the prunes. Each iteration of the cake is distinct and luscious.

2 large eggs

½ cup (1 stick) soft, unsalted butter

1 cup firmly packed dark brown sugar

1½ cups cake flour

1 teaspoon baking powder

½ teaspoon salt

1 teaspoon ground cinnamon

½ teaspoon ground cloves

½ teaspoon ground nutmeg

½ cup milk

4 ounces pitted prunes, chopped (about 1 cup)

1 cup golden raisins

1. PREPARE TO BAKE. Arrange the rack in the center of the oven and preheat it to 400° F. Spritz one 9-by-5-inch shiny aluminum loaf pan and the shiny side of a piece of aluminum foil large enough to cover the top of the pan with Baker's Joy. Place the unbroken eggs in a bowl of hot tap water.

2. MAKE THE BATTER. Cream the butter until light, then add the brown sugar and beat well. Add the eggs, one at a time, beating well. Sift the flour, baking powder, salt, cinnamon, cloves, and nutmeg on a sheet of wax paper, then add to the creamed mixture in thirds, alternately with the milk, beating just until mixed. Fold in the prunes and raisins.

3. BAKE THE CAKE. Pour the batter into the prepared pan, cover loosely with the foil, shiny side down, and bake for 25 minutes. Quickly whisk off the foil and continue baking until a wooden pick comes out clean, about 20 more minutes. Cool in the pan on a rack for 5 minutes, then flip it out onto the rack to cool. Store wrapped in plastic wrap.

pumpkin nut loaf cake

Dense and delicious, this cake is lovely when toasted and served with a smear of mascarpone for afternoon tea.

baker's tip

Can't find canned pumpkin? Look in the baking aisle of the supermarket. Still none? Substitute a fresh sweet potato or winter squash. Pierce and microwave until tender, about 10 minutes. Cut in half, cool, and then scrape out and discard the seeds. Then scrape and mash the flesh of the squash with a fork.

2 large eggs

2 cups sifted cake flour

2 teaspoons pumpkin pie spice

2 teaspoons baking powder

1 teaspoon salt

½ teaspoon baking soda

1 (15-ounce) can pumpkin

1 cup firmly packed dark brown sugar

½ cup whipping cream

2 tablespoons unsalted butter, melted

½ cup chopped walnuts

1. PREPARE TO BAKE. Arrange the rack in the middle of the oven and preheat it to 400°F. Spritz a 9-by-5-inch shiny aluminum loaf pan and the shiny side of a piece of aluminum foil large enough to cover the top of the pan with Baker's Joy. Place the unbroken eggs in a bowl of hot tap water.

2. MAKE THE BATTER. Stir the flour, pie spice, baking powder, salt, and baking soda together in a large bowl. Whisk together the eggs, pumpkin, brown sugar, cream, and melted butter in a glass measure. Pour into the flour mixture and mix just until moistened.

3. BAKE THE CAKE. Pour the batter into the prepared pan and top with the chopped nuts. Cover loosely with the foil, shiny side down, and bake for 25 minutes. Quickly whisk off the foil and continue to bake until a wooden pick comes out clean, 20 to 25 more minutes. Cool in the pan on a rack for 5 minutes, then flip it out onto the rack to cool completely. Store tightly wrapped in plastic.

8

Candy Bar
CAKES

Caterers have long known that candy bar cakes are among their clients' top choices. Sweeter than most cakes with the added concentration of sugar from the candy, they are amazingly popular for bridal showers, weddings, and celebrations for kids.

baby ruth layer cake

Here's the All-American cousin to a German chocolate cake. Buy a 1.75-pound bag of fun-size Baby Ruth candy bars, start stripping them out of the wrappers, and soon you'll have the basis of a cake made popular by West Coast caterers, who say their customers order and reorder these candy bar cakes for wedding showers and birthday parties. The cake looks for all the world like a German chocolate cake, but has that unforgettable Baby Ruth flavor that I grew up on.

baker's tip Use a microwave to melt the candy bars—they'll be done in 30 seconds—or simply throw them into the top of a double boiler. Either way, you quickly have a flavorful cake and frosting addition.

2 large eggs

12 fun-size Baby Ruth candy bars, cut in half (from a 1.75-pound bag)

¼ cup chunky peanut butter

6 tablespoons half-and-half

1¼ cups granulated sugar

½ cup (1 stick) soft, unsalted butter

1 teaspoon vanilla extract

2 cups sifted cake flour

2½ tablespoons confectioners' sugar

1 teaspoon baking soda

½ teaspoon baking powder

1 cup buttermilk

1. PREPARE TO BAKE. Arrange the rack in the middle of the oven and preheat it to 400°F. Spritz three 8-inch shiny round aluminum cake pans with Baker's Joy. Place the unbroken eggs in a bowl of hot tap water. Combine the candy bars, peanut butter, and half-and-half in the top of a double boiler or microwave and heat, stirring until melted and blended, about 1 minute in the microwave or 3 minutes in a double boiler.

2. MAKE THE BATTER. Cream the granulated sugar and butter in a stand mixer until fluffy, adding the eggs, one at a time, near the end. Blend in the melted candy and vanilla. Sift the flour, confectioners' sugar, baking soda, and baking powder onto a piece of wax paper. Spoon the flour mixture into the butter mixture in thirds, alternately with the buttermilk. Mix on low speed just until blended.

3. BAKE THE CAKE. Divide the batter evenly among the pans and bake until a wooden pick comes out clean, 15 to 20 minutes. Cool in the pans on a rack for 5 minutes, then flip out onto the rack to finish cooling.

FROSTING

10 fun-size Baby Ruth candy bars, cut in half

2 large egg yolks

1 cup half-and-half

1 cup sugar

⅛ teaspoon salt

½ cup (1 stick) unsalted butter

2 cups sweetened, flaked coconut

½ cup salted peanuts, chopped

4. MAKE THE FROSTING. Melt the candy bars in the top of a double boiler or in a microwave (1 minute in a microwave, 2 minutes in a double boiler). Stir to mix. Combine the egg yolks, half-and-half, sugar, salt, and butter in a medium saucepan. Cook and stir until thick, about 6 minutes. Remove from the heat and stir in the melted candy, coconut, and peanuts. Cool, then beat vigorously with a wooden spoon.

5. ASSEMBLE THE CAKE. Place one cake layer on a cake stand, then spread frosting generously on top. Repeat with the remaining 2 layers, covering the top of each. Cut carefully with a sharp knife. Store under a cake bell.

butterfinger cheesecake

New York meets the Midwest in this candy bar cheesecake. It's yummy. It's easy. It takes almost an hour to bake and a while to cool, but it's worth it.

baker's tip { Dip a long, thin-bladed knife in hot water before cutting this cake and you'll get nice, even cuts for a picture-perfect wedge.

CRUST

1 cup graham cracker crumbs

¼ cup sugar

1 (2.16-ounce) Butterfinger candy bar, crushed in a food processor

¼ cup unsalted butter, melted

FILLING

16 ounces cream cheese

2 teaspoons vanilla extract

1¼ cups sugar

3 large eggs

1 cup sour cream

1 (2.16-ounce) Butterfinger candy bar, crushed in a food processor

1. **PREPARE TO BAKE.** Arrange the rack in the middle of the oven and preheat it to 350°F. Place the eggs for the filling in a bowl of hot tap water.

2. **MAKE THE CRUST.** Preheat the oven to 350°F. Combine the graham cracker crumbs, sugar, and Butterfinger crumbs in a 9-inch springform pan. Drizzle the melted butter over all and stir to mix. Press down with the back of a spoon to form a crust that covers the bottom and comes 1½ inches up the side of the pan. Bake for 6 minutes, then set aside.

3. **MAKE THE FILLING.** Add the cream cheese to the mixer bowl and whip to soften, adding the vanilla, sugar, eggs (one at a time), and sour cream. Fold in half of the crushed Butterfinger bars and pour the mixture into the crust.

4. **BAKE THE CAKE** until the center is set, 40 to 55 minutes. Turn off the oven. Leaving the door slightly ajar, leave the cheesecake in the oven for 1 hour. Remove from the oven and sprinkle with the remaining crushed Butterfinger bars. Refrigerate, covered.

5. **TO SERVE,** remove the sides of the pan and place the cake on a serving plate, leaving the bottom of the pan in place. Cut into thin slices.

hershey's kisses mini-cupcakes

Good things come in small packages, and provided you have the patience to unwrap 48 Hershey's Kisses without eating them, you can make a luscious little bite of a cake with a kiss in the middle. Mini-cupcakes will bake in 7 or 8 minutes, standard ones in 10 minutes. Hold one in your hand and you'll see a little daisy of a cake, with golden cake enveloping the kiss that's nestled in the middle. Each mini-cupcake is one perfect bite. Trust me on this: The kiss is all the finish that's required.

baker's tip

To properly fill cupcake or mini-cupcake pans, measure out the batter. Two tablespoons will scoop out just the right amount of batter for a mini-cupcake; a ¼-cup measuring cup holds the correct amount for a regular cupcake pan.

¾ cup (1½ sticks) soft, unsalted butter

1 cup sugar

2 large egg yolks

2 cups sifted cake flour

1 tablespoon baking powder

¾ cup milk

48 Hershey's kisses, unwrapped

1. PREPARE TO BAKE. Arrange the rack in the middle of the oven and preheat it to 400°F. Line 48 mini-cupcake cups or 24 standard cups with foil papers, or spritz with Baker's Joy and set aside. Place the unbroken eggs in a bowl of hot tap water.

2. MAKE THE BATTER. Cream the butter and sugar in a stand mixer until light. Add the egg yolks, one at a time, and beat until well incorporated. Add the flour and baking powder to this mixture in thirds, alternately with the milk. Stop beating when the mixture is well blended.

3. BAKE THE CAKES. Drop the batter into the prepared cups. filling them two-thirds full. Into the center of each, place a Hershey's kiss. Bake until golden, 7 to 8 minutes for mini-cupcakes and 10 minutes for standard ones. Cool on a rack. Store in an airtight tin.

payday candy bar cake

If you loved that chewy peanut roll when you were a kid and would like to show your children something old that's new again, whip up this so-called cake in half an hour. Let it cool, and then cut it into small squares. This is retro to the max. You may wonder why it's not called a Reese's Peanut Butter cake, since it has no Payday candy and does have Reese's peanut butter chips. Just make it. You'll see. This is a great project for 10-year-olds who want to start cooking.

baker's tip
> For a great Boy or Girl Scout project, get the kids to make these cakes and then wrap them in clear plastic. Mark 'em at a buck apiece and sell them at the bake sale. They'll be coming back for more.

1 large egg

¾ cup (1½ sticks) unsalted butter, divided

2 cups sifted cake flour

2 teaspoons baking powder

½ teaspoon salt

1 cup sugar

3 cups miniature marshmallows

1 (10-ounce) package Reese's peanut butter chips

1⅔ cups light corn syrup

2 teaspoons vanilla extract

1½ cups crisp rice cereal (such as Rice Krispies)

2 cups roasted, salted peanuts

1. **PREPARE TO BAKE.** Arrange the rack in the middle of the oven and preheat it to 400°F. Place the egg in a bowl of hot tap water. In a glass measure or medium saucepan, melt ½ cup of the butter in the microwave or on the stovetop.

2. **MAKE THE CAKE.** In a 9-by-13-inch glass baking pan, combine the melted butter, egg, flour, baking powder, salt, and sugar. Stir with your hands to moisten, then pat down to make a crust. Bake until lightly browned, 10 to 12 minutes. Open the oven door, lift out the crust, and top with the marshmallows. Spread them evenly over the top of the crust and replace in the oven for 2 to 3 minutes, or until the marshmallows begin to puff and brown. Remove to a rack to cool.

3. **MAKE THE TOPPING.** While the crust is baking, melt the remaining ¼ cup butter, peanut butter chips, and corn syrup in the pan or a microwavable bowl until the chips have melted, about 1 minute. Stir in the vanilla, rice cereal, and peanuts. Stir to coat the peanuts. Spoon the peanut butter mixture over the top of the puffed marshmallows. Cool and cut into 24 squares.

peppermint patty's new year's cheesecake

Combining the flavor of peppermints with best-quality bittersweet chocolate in a refrigerator cheese-cake provides a bittersweet taste sensation. This cake makes good use of those peppermint candy canes you put on the Christmas tree and hate to throw away. If you don't have any, use hard peppermint candies. Make the cake the day before you're planning to serve it to give the flavors a chance to marry.

baker's tip

> The simplest way to smash the peppermints is to place them in a resealable plastic bag and smack them with a hammer. Turn the bag over, shake it, and hit it again. Before you know it, you'll have shards of peppermints to use.

¼ cup (½ stick) unsalted butter

1 cup Nabisco Chocolate Wafer crumbs (about 20 wafers)

1 envelope unflavored gelatin

¼ cup cold water

19 ounces soft cream cheese (two 8-ounce packages and one 3-ounce package)

½ cup sugar

½ cup milk

½ cup crushed peppermint candy, divided

1½ cups whipping cream

2 best-quality bittersweet chocolate bars (1.45 ounces each), finely chopped, divided

1. PREPARE TO BAKE. Preheat the oven to 350°F. Melt the butter in the microwave for 30 seconds, then combine the crumbs and butter in a 9-inch springform pan and press the mixture down along the bottom and up the sides. Bake for 10 minutes. Cool.

2. MAKE THE CAKE. Soften the gelatin in the water in a small saucepan. Stir over low heat until dissolved. Combine the cream cheese and sugar in a stand mixer, mixing at medium speed until well blended. Gradually pour in the gelatin mixture, milk, and half of the peppermint candy, mixing until blended. Chill until thickened but not set. Meanwhile, whip the cream until soft peaks form. Set ¾ cup of the whipped cream and ½ cup of the chopped chocolate aside. Fold the remaining whipped cream and chocolate into the gelatin mixture and pour over the cooked and cooled crust.

3. FINISH THE CAKE. Chill until firm. Garnish with the reserved whipped cream folded with the remaining crushed peppermint candy, and sprinkle with the remaining chocolate.

mail-order sources

PROVISIONING THE BAKER'S KITCHEN

New materials, old materials, here are a few of my favorite things for baking:

Shiny aluminum pans. Cook's Dream stocks aluminum pans of every size and description. These were good enough for my mother in the forties, and they're still the very best. Durable, inexpensive, and they work as advertised. They heat up quickly, they cool down quickly, they provide a surface to brown cakes and leave a lovely crumb while being free of any hot spots or raw-dough spots. Order online at www.Cooksdream.com.

Silpat. This amazing silicone impregnated cloth mat, 11⅝ x 16½ inches, goes into the bottom of the jelly roll pan instead of parchment in many recipes. It is so easy to use. Just plop it in the pan, add cake batter. Bake, then peel the baked cake off the cloth. Perfect for jelly rolls.

Because it's made of silicone, nothing sticks to it—not even peanut brittle. This mat sits easily in a 13-x-18-inch sheet pan and is completely safe for use in an oven or freezer. Finished baking that jelly roll? Simply tip over the tray and the cake can be easily removed. Wipe clean and you are ready for the next cake. This highly useful mat will prove itself invaluable again and again. Purchase at your local kitchen store or order from www.chefdepot.net or www.demarleusa.com.

Microplane. This is the best hand-tool to hit the baker's circuit in years. This wand with the patented surface will grate chocolate, nutmeg, cinnamon, lemons, or just about anything else you need to make that cake. Drop it in the dishwasher until tomorrow. I use mine every day. One of those better mousetrap ideas. So easy, you'll say "Why didn't I think of

that." Only caveat—accept no substitutes. Some rather well-known high-end chains sell copies and imitations. They don't work as well. Purchase at your local kitchen store or order online at www.microplane.com.

Silicone Bakeware. Available only to professional bakers and at a high cost for years, now you can purchase bakeware made from silicone that makes baking a snap. Not to be confused with the stuff of computer chips, silicone is the stuff that makes bakeware supple and heat resistant to 500° F, yet super non-stick. Freezer and microwave safe, it's sold in every size and style from cupcake to super Madeline to sexy Bundt pans. These pans bake everything well. They won't give you that crisp, brown crust you can get from shiny aluminum—but they're so easy, you won't care. If they feel a bit too much like a rubber chicken to you when filled with batter, place them on a cookie sheet for easy maneuverability into and out of the oven. Purchase at your local kitchen store or order online at www.kitchencollection.com.

Fancy Paper Goods. OK. So you want to present your baked cakes and cupcakes in professional paper ware? No problem. Order your own pink boxes, paper circles for the bottoms of the cakes as well as enough fanciful paper ware to transport cakes to keep your mind racing for months. Order online at www.papermart.com.

Stand Mixers. Yes, you'll want one of these, and, no, you don't need to spend $300 to get one. Using an old-fashioned Hamilton Beach model with two bowls (one small bowl and one narrow, tall bowl is perfect for whipping up egg whites and seven minute icing), I wrote the entire book without once using my trusty KitchenAid. Although KitchenAid is the gold standard, you can certainly get by with the old-fashioned two-bowl kind. Beyond Hamilton Beach, there is the trusty Sunbeam Mixmaster, now known as the "Heritage" model, with two stainless steel bowls, and now available at places like Walmart for less than $100. If your heart belongs with Mrs. Cleaver, this is the mixer for you. Purchase at your local Walmart or other local department store, or order online at www.kitchenaid.com or www.walmart.com.

Ribbon Candy. A variety of ribbon candy and other candies perfect for cake decorating can be found online at www.candy4U.com.

Food Coloring. Cool colors for creating fabulous decorative icings can be found at the Wilton Store. From vibrant primary colors to pastels and garden shades, this store also stocks a wide variety of cake-baking tools and accessories. Order online at www.wilton.com.

Flavorings. Nutrition Lifestyles offers Blue Cattle Truck Mexican vanilla, the brand I recommend whenever a recipe calls for vanilla. Purchase at 888-227-5395 or order online at www.nutritionlifestyles.com.

For delicious orange oil and other flavorings, from cinnamon to raspberry to spearmint, Boyajian is the place to go. Order online at www.boyajianinc.com.

Cookware. I often recommend Le Creuset cookware, especially the saucepan with the lip for easy pouring. Le Creuset can be found at many national kitchen stores and department stores. Check out their Web site at www.lecreuset.com for more information.

Bakeware. For a variety of bakeware and cake baking supplies, from lovely paper cups to unusual Bundt pans, call 866-862-CHEF or order online at www.kitchenconservatory.com.

Bundt pans can also be ordered directly from NordicWare through their toll-free number 877-466-7342. See their Web site at www.nordicware.com.

Chocolate. Most of the chocolate brands I recommend, Droste, Lindt, Toblerone, and Ghiradelli can be found in your local supermarket or gourmet grocery. Online sources include www.ghiradelli.com; www.toblerone.com; www.lindt.com; and this great site, www.chocolatesource.com, for an even wider array of choices.

Spices. One of the best sources for excellent spices is Penzeys. Order online at www.penzeys.com.

index

table of equivalents

The exact equivalents in the following tables have been rounded for convenience.

LIQUID/DRY MEASURES

U.S.	METRIC
¼ teaspoon	1.25 milliliters
½ teaspoon	2.5 milliliters
1 teaspoon	5 milliliters
1 tablespoon (3 teaspoons)	15 milliliters
1 fluid ounce (2 tablespoons)	30 milliliters
¼ cup	60 milliliters
⅓ cup	80 milliliters
½ cup	120 milliliters
1 cup	240 milliliters
1 pint (2 cups)	480 milliliters
1 quart (4 cups, 32 ounces)	960 milliliters
1 gallon (4 quarts)	3.84 liters
1 ounce (by weight)	28 grams
1 pound	454 grams
2.2 pounds	1 kilogram

OVEN TEMPERATURE

FAHRENHEIT	CELSIUS	GAS
250	120	½
275	140	1
300	150	2
325	160	3
350	180	4
375	190	5
400	200	6
425	220	7
450	230	8
475	240	9
500	260	10

LENGTH

U.S.	METRIC
⅛ inch	3 millimeters
¼ inch	6 millimeters
½ inch	12 millimeters
1 inch	2.5 centimeters